"Very few books a *and business stewar~~a~~.* Compound Effect *speaks of transformational the power to marketplace. Whether you're running a large corporation, small business, non-profit organization or church, the material Dan provides will have a deep and lasting impact. I've incorporated many of the principles and I believe after reading this you'll be doing the same."*

— Gary Wilkerson, Senior
Pastor – **The Springs Church**
(www.thespringschurch.com)
President – **World Challenge**
(www.worldchallenge.org)

"We've all seen enough shoddy fish-on-the-van businesses. The Compound Effect *navigates the oft-muddied waters of "Christian business" with razor-sharp clarity and refreshing honesty, challenging God's people to increase the Kingdom Impact of our enterprises. Dan's book articulates what his life proclaims: The marketplace is a mission field to be navigated with spiritual fervor and professional excellence."*

— Rob Brendle, Senior Pastor,
Denver United Church

"Dan Meylan has identified the two critical elements of impacting the marketplace—spiritual maturity and business competency. Putting the two together results in a compounding witness for Jesus Christ that is irrefutable. He has written

a book that is challenging and extremely practical, however, it calls for a lifetime commitment. You will be encouraged, empowered, and equipped for ministry on Main Street or Wall Street as you take to heart what he has written.

It is my privilege to endorse this book."

— Ron Blue, Founder
Kingdom Advisors
www.kingdomadvisors.com

"In my fifty years of combined leadership experience in both the business and Christian community, I have had numerous opportunities to share on the subject of effective marketplace ministry. I only wish I would have met Dan Meylan a lot earlier. What he has discovered, and so artfully unpacks in The Compound Effect, takes most of what I understood about this important topic to another universe. This book is critical given the condition of our business culture today and a must-read for every Christian."

— Vince D'Acchioli, Founder,
On Target Ministries
www.ontargetinstitute.org

"I have a great number of business books and manuals on my bookshelves and, as a chaplain/minister, I also have an exhaustive theological library. Never have I seen a single volume, which properly integrates the spiritual dimension with core business competencies. Dan Meylan's book, The Compound Effect, is just such a book. Dan's background

*in business and banking uniquely qualifies him to speak
authoritatively to business leaders regarding transferable
business principles, which apply to mom-and-pop shops as
well as Fortune 100 global corporations. The intentional inte-
gration of biblical principles and growth toward spiritual
maturity equips leaders to successfully impact the world. "*

— Jay W. Badry,
Marketplace Chaplains USA
www.mchapusa.com

"The Compound Effect *brings illumination to the mysteri-
ous seed of God within each of us that desires to grow and
mature us in the destiny for which we have been created.
Daniel Meylan reveals his own significant journey while
using timeless practical principles that lead readers toward
godly successful living. You will begin to see a more integrat-
ed life based on who you really are, and how much potential
impact you have in what you are called to do. As the Spirit
leads you through this guide, expect a fuller fusion with God,
and the world around you."*

— Robert Ricciardelli,
Converging Zone Network
www.covergingzone.com

*"Dan's business background brings a great balance
between wisdom and revelation to marketplace ministry.
Most of us come from a revelation-only church background
and we're not sure how to navigate in the kingdom. We're*

not leaving revelation or gifts behind; we're just adding a new measure of spirituality called "wealth creation." And the wealth created in business isn't just being given away. These kingdom businessmen are converting money into ministry and teaching a new generation how to create their own wealth—self-sustaining missions that impact cultures and "disciple nations." These kingdom pioneers in marketplace ministry are starting with the desires in their own hearts and spending a lifetime having fun, making money, and loving people. You're invited."

— John Garfield, author
Releasing Kings
www.releasing-kings.com

"It is easier to train a gifted marketplace leader how to walk with God than it is to train a missionary how to effectively lead a business. Daniel Meylan helps us to do both. Get this book, read it, and do it for The Compound Effect.*"*

— Kent Humphreys, Ambassador
FCCI / Christ@Work

"I have read Dan's new book and it is outstanding! WOW! It's full of advice and wisdom you can't afford not to listen and implement into your business. I highly recommend it

It's by far one of the best books I have read in a longtime. It's a must for anyone seeking direction in their business and their spiritual life! GREAT JOB!"

— Jim Dismore
Kingdom Way Companies

THE COMPOUND EFFECT

THE COMPOUND EFFECT

THE TRANSFORMATIONAL POWER OF BUSINESS COMPETENCY & SPIRITUAL MATURITY

by
DANIEL MEYLAN

dawson media

THE COMPOUND EFFECT: THE TRANSFORMATIONAL POWER OF BUSINESS COMPETENCY & SPIRITUAL MATURITY

ISBN: 978-1-93565-1-109

Cover design by Design Corps, www.designcorps.us

Cover illustration by John Wollinka, photography from iStock Images

LCCN: 2011926512
Printed in the United States of America
15 14 13 12 11   1 2 3 4 5 6 7 8

DEDICATION:

This book is dedicated to my wife, Kathy,
a victorious warrior for the ages.

ANALYSIS SHEET

THE COMPOUND EFFECT

CONTENTS:

This work is the sum and substance of a lifetime of learning, experiences, relationships, triumphs, and tragedies. But most importantly it is the product of prayer and, only a very small portion of it, my prayers. It would be easy and appropriate for me to acknowledge my family, my many coaches, teachers, mentors, and friends who walked with me through childhood, adolescence, schooling, early business ventures and, later, significant business accomplishments who would serve as the foundation for this book. But none of those acknowledgments would have mattered and this work would not have been birthed without the fervent and righteous prayers of numerous men and women. During a time when my life was seriously flawed and on course for total destruction, a group of godly, humble, imperfect men came around me and loved me in a way I never knew, a Christlike way. They lifted me through prayer and serious, no-nonsense, loving accountability. Unbeknownst to me at the time, I also became the prayer assignment of a number of incredible godly intercessors. I now know and understand, more than a decade later, the depth and fervor of their prayers and petitions on my behalf. One person in particular, my wife, Kathy, carried the cause of my life's purpose as a husband, father, man, and leader before God more often than I will ever know. She loved me unconditionally by and through her prayers. This work is the fruit of the thousands of seeds of prayer planted by Kathy and many others. From these powerful prayer warriors I learned this valuable wisdom:

Prayer changes hearts.

Changed hearts come to repentance and then change behaviors.

Changed behaviors change habits.

Changed habits change lifestyles.

Changed lifestyles change outcomes.

If this book encourages you to dream and your visions are lofty, be advised the obstacles are usually loftier. Prayer removes obstacles and cultivates dreams into transformational legacies. This book is proof of the purpose and power of prayer.

INTRODUCTION

You are my portion, O LORD;
I have promised to obey your words.
I have sought your face with
all my heart; be gracious to me
according to your promise.

— Psalm 119:56-58

distinctly remember the day I was saved. I was under a great deal of stress about finances, relationships, my education, and my future. A very close friend had been witnessing diligently to me for some time, trying to make me understand the power of the love of Christ and the difference it would make in my life.

That day, as I sat on the floor of my friend's living room and gave my heart to the Lord, my first sensation was an incredible release of tension and stress. It was as though an enormous load had been lifted from my shoulders—Someone had miraculously removed it. And in that single moment, the course of my entire life changed direction. I was transformed forever.

What my friend did, by sharing the love of Christ with me, is the highest calling and purpose any of us can fulfill. Jesus said to His disciples (and to us as well), "Therefore go and make disciples of all nations, baptizing them in the name of the Father and of the Son and of the Holy Spirit, and teaching them to obey everything I have commanded you" (Matthew 28:19-20). How do we reach the lost? Practically speaking, how do we go and make disciples of all nations? How do you and I, in our everyday lives, carry out the Great Commission?

Many Christians believe that to truly be a minister of the gospel they must serve in full-time ministry in a local church or on the mission field. But, if you are like me, you are most likely called to sow seeds of faith and labor for the harvest in the marketplace. The numbers tell the story—in the United States alone, there are 13.75 million private sector companies that employ 120,600,000 people. All religious organizations (including churches, ministries, and organizations that have adopted a "religious purpose") represent just 2.62 percent of all private sector companies, 1.4 percent of all employed persons and .61 percent of all payroll. That means that approximately 98.4 percent of Christians today are investing their time, talents, and energy in the business world.

With so many of us sent out into the marketplace, why aren't we seeing greater results for the kingdom of God? Why aren't more Christian business owners and organizations on the forefront of relevancy in our culture? The unfortunate truth is that there are countless poorly operated Christian businesses that are creating devastating collateral damage to the body of Christ because of their incompetence, lack of training, lack of knowledge, and inexperience.

The other problem? Too many believers are simply not growing in their walk with God. Their spiritual lives take a backseat to other priorities—or at least are left behind during the workweek. Rarely do we find the business owner who operates with business competency *and* spiritual maturity. But both are necessary to succeed in bringing transformation and change to our world. And the impact that occurs when these two elements come together and are multiplied is phenomenal.

This book is a lifetime road map for entrepreneurs,

emerging business owners, and established business leaders with specific directions to grow, thrive, and profit while serving the Lord—and thereby changing the world. You will find directions, mile markers, and signposts for both the business and spiritual aspects of operating a kingdom-serving enterprise.

The greatest opportunity to harness God's power to transform the world is through the Christian business community. The potential is endless and the need is great—this is the final frontier for the body of Christ. The reality is that vibrant, growing, profitable businesses built upon kingdom principles and committed to divine stewardship of their resources have far more capability to transform their community, their nation, and the world than the corporate church. This is the critical message of *The Compound Effect*—that *your business is your ministry.*

CHAPTER 1

THE ABILITY TO TRANSFORM

Therefore, I urge you, brothers, in view of God's mercy, to offer your bodies as living sacrifices, holy and pleasing to God—this is your spiritual act of worship. Do not conform any longer to the pattern of this world, but be transformed by the renewing of your mind. Then you will be able to test and approve what God's will is—his good, pleasing and perfect will.

— Romans 12:1-2

In this modern age of instant information and an exploding global marketplace, many believers are seeking to understand how business and ministry can effectively coexist. Faced with widespread economic struggles, today's Christian small-business owners find themselves under intense pressure to get beyond survival mode and reach new levels of growth and achievement. Many are looking for answers and solutions to their operational business issues, however, road maps to success that use biblical principles have been scarce or nonexistent.

At the same time, many church and ministry leaders are struggling to find ways to effectively apply business principles to their organizations. But because of their lack of understanding about how the business community thinks and acts, pastors and ministry leaders are often disconnected from the marketplace—and the unlimited resources it represents.

> Ministry is about the transformation of people's lives.

What so many believers—both in church leadership and the marketplace—have failed to understand is that *your business is your ministry*. In recent years, awareness of this truth has begun to come to the forefront within some Christian circles. But really, this is not a new concept. Ministry, as demonstrated through the life of Jesus Christ, is not about possessing a pastoral job description or seminary degree, or being aligned with an association of churches. Ministry is about the transformation of people's lives. Jesus did not operate His ministry within the four walls of a church or temple. His disciples came directly from the real world, not a seminary. And each of them had a specific business skill and functional understanding of the marketplace.

Business owners have a unique opportunity to directly impact and transform lives on multiple levels—including their families, employees, customers, vendors, suppliers, and communities. The extent of influence they can achieve in the business world today is unmatched—even by the church. It crosses all cultural and language barriers, extending from local communities, through small and large cities, and out into the nations of the world.

All business involves relationships. All ministry involves relationships. The effectiveness and success of both business and ministry is directly dependent on the quality and depth of our relationships. As business owners, we build and sustain relationships every day. However, we cannot hope to establish quality marketplace relationships without first being competent in the manner in which our business is operated.

God's expectation is for all people to be transformed by the gospel of Christ. As Christian business owners, we have an incredible opportunity to evangelize and transform lives for the kingdom of God. If our business is run with competence, our relationships and influence will expand. But if we are not competent and our business is poorly run, we will lose influence, undermine and diminish our relationships, and ultimately fail.

The Power of Multiplication

The economy of God's kingdom has always operated on the principle of the multiplication of resources according to His plans and provisions. Jesus taught on this subject often, saying, "Others, like seed sown on good soil, hear the word, accept it, and produce a crop—some thirty, some sixty, some a hundred times what was sown" (Mark 4:20). The "crop" that we produce, the fruit of the labor in our lives, will always be a result of the multiplication of resources that have been invested—both spiritual and natural.

The Compound Effect is a stewardship concept that establishes a direct correlation between spiritual maturity and business competency. How and where spiritual maturity and business competency intersect determines the level of transformation we will be able to accomplish in the lives of others. Understanding how these practical business and spiritual attributes combine is the critical key to enable business owners to achieve their full potential and, in the process, transform lives, communities, and nations.

When our level of business competency is multiplied by our degree of spiritual maturity, the resulting value measures our "Kingdom Impact." We define Kingdom Impact as our ability to transform the lives of the people within our sphere of influence through the application and demonstration of Christ's love and biblical principles. We will explore the concept of Kingdom Impact in greater depth in the next chapter. But it is important that we understand that The Compound Effect defines, measures, and illustrates Kingdom Impact. It is a quantitative measure of our effectiveness as Christian business owners and ministry leaders in achieving God's desired transformation of people's lives.

Our purpose is to define and measure the growth and effectiveness of our Kingdom Impact in the lives of those who come in contact with our businesses and ministries. The stronger our business competency and the greater our spiritual maturity, the higher the level of our Kingdom Impact. The Compound Effect process will allow you and your organization to understand how to develop and grow in such a way that you can consistently expand and improve your level of transformational Kingdom Impact.

The Process of Maturing

In both biblical and natural contexts, the process of development and growth is referred to as *maturing*. God established His kingdom on earth with the design that all life would involve birth, growth, learning, and physical death. This process of maturing occurs not only with people and nature, but also within organizations. Fortunately, there are many Scriptures that address this important principle.

Until we all reach unity in the faith and in the knowledge of the Son of God and become mature, attaining to the whole measure of the fullness of Christ.

—Ephesians 4:13

*I press on toward the goal to win the prize for
which God has called me heavenward in Christ
Jesus. All of us, then, who are mature should take
such a view of things.*

—Philippians 3:14-15

*But solid food is for the mature, who by constant use
have trained themselves to distinguish good from evil.*

—Hebrews 5:14

*Let perseverance finish its work so that you may be
mature and complete, not lacking anything.*

—James 1:4

*For this very reason, make every effort to add to your
faith goodness; and to goodness, knowledge; and to
knowledge, self-control; and to self-control, perseverance; and to perseverance, godliness; and to godliness,
mutual affection; and to mutual affection, love. For if
you possess these qualities in increasing measure, they
will keep you from being ineffective and unproductive
in your knowledge of our Lord Jesus Christ.*

—2 Peter 1:5-8

The key words in this last Scripture are "to add to" and "in
increasing measure," which imply maturing. The warning that
we must heed is that if we fail "to add to," we will become
unproductive and ineffective in our knowledge of Jesus Christ
and our ability to improve His kingdom here on earth.

Spiritual maturity is a lifetime process of learning and applying the principles of righteousness that God demonstrated through the life of Christ as described in the Bible. Business competency is the process of maturing in the knowledge and skills required to effectively operate a business, organization, or ministry.

Measuring business competency and spiritual maturity involves creating definitions of specific behaviors that reflect where we are as individuals and organizations. These definitions contrast and quantify distinct and identifiable behaviors that are easily recognized. The Compound Effect establishes three primary categories of behavioral definitions in the business arena:

The **Survivor**

The **Successful**

The **Significant**

These three business categories serve as the cornerstone of The Compound Effect. Here is one example of how these three behavioral categories are differentiated. Which one are you?

The **Survivor** *business begs for customers.*

The **Successful** *business selects customers.*

The **Significant** *business creates customers.*

In measuring the component of spiritual maturity we have defined three primary behavioral categories as well.

They are:

The **User**

The **Servant**

The **Leader**

Here is an example of these three behavioral categories and how they might be differentiated in the area of relationships. Which one are you?

The **User** – *It's about me and Jesus.*

The **Servant** – *It's about you and Jesus.*

The **Leader** – *It's about Jesus and His kingdom.*

These are very brief examples of how we define the behavioral stages of business competency and spiritual maturity. For the purposes of making more detailed distinctions of the characteristics within these three business and spiritual categories, we have further defined each category by more than twenty separate comparisons of behaviors and provided narrative illustrations that represent examples of the differences in each behavior.

Each business category has been assigned a numerical value in order to reflect your business competency and skills and the capabilities of your organization. The Survivor is assigned a numerical ranking from 1 to 3, the Successful is given a numerical ranking from 4 to 6, and the Significant receives a numerical ranking from 7 to 10. We will discuss the final numerical assignment process in more detail later in the text, but the following table provides the basic scale of measurement.

The Compound Effect Business Competence Scale

0 = **No knowledge or competence**

1-3 = **Emerging competence**

   1 = I have read about this subject.

   2 = Someone has told me about this subject.

   3 = I have started to understand this subject.

4-6 = **Adequate competence**

   4 = I have started doing this.

   5 = I understand how this applies in my business.

   6 = I am comfortable with this skill.

7-10 = **Strong Competence**

   7 = This is one of my strongest skills.

   8 = I can teach others this skill.

   9 = My peers seek my advice on this subject.

   10 = I have a global reputation as a subject-matter expert in this area.

Similarly, your spiritual maturity is measured by a numerical value scale that assigns a value from 1 to 3 for the User, from 4 to 6 for the Servant, and from 7 to 10 for the Leader.

The Compound Effect Spiritual Maturity Scale

0 = **I am not saved** – I do not have a personal relationship with Christ.

1-3 = **User**

　1 = I am saved and trying to figure out my life.

　2 = I am saved and I am looking to God for answers.

　3 = I am saved and finding answers from God.

4-6 = **Servant**

　4 = I am reading the Bible and trying to apply what it says.

　5 = I am studying the Bible and changing my behaviors.

　6 = I am using the Bible as a reference point for my actions and attitudes.

7-10 = **Leader**

　7 = I know the Bible and promote biblical principles.

　8 = I know God's heart and anticipate His requirements.

　9 = I am obedient to God's voice without regard to myself.

　10 = I am prepared to sacrifice all, even unto death, for the cause of Christ.

When the numerical value of business competency is multiplied by the numerical value of spiritual maturity, the resulting number is a representative indication of the current Kingdom Impact of the individual or organization.

The stronger the business competency and the deeper the spiritual maturity, the greater the Kingdom Impact of the business owner or ministry leader and their enterprise.

The Businessman

Don is a fifty-four-year-old business executive. He is a competent business owner and owns and operates a chain of convenience stores with sixteen locations in two states. Don founded his company in 1982 and now employs more than one hundred people and generates $40 million in gross annual sales. All of his stores are owned, not rented, and only seven of the sixteen still have a mortgage. The margins are small and the competition is fierce. Don's greatest challenge is finding qualified competent managers and staff for his stores. He has eight key managers who have been with him at least ten years, but he is always on the lookout for new talent. All his key managers participate in a company-wide profit-sharing plan which enables them to earn six-figure incomes. Thanks in part to his thirty years of retail experience and his tight operating systems, Don's company generates more than $700,000 in after-tax income annually. The current market value of the equity in Don's commercial real estate is $7.7 million and growing at the rate of $500,000 per year. By using The Compound Effect Business Competency Scale to measure Don's business skills and abilities, his business competence was scored as an 8.1 on a scale of 0-10.

Don and his wife, Evie, have five children, one of whom is disabled as the result of an automobile accident involving a drunk driver. Don and Evie are members of a local Bible church but only attend every third or fourth Sunday due to family, ministry, and business commitments. Don serves on the board of directors for a large evangelical global relief organization established by his wife's family in the 1950s. This ministry takes full advantage of Don's keen attention to detail and systems. He travels extensively and spends as much time with this global relief organization as he does with his own business.

Don and Evie are long-standing members of a couples' prayer group that has been meeting weekly for many years. These couples meet collectively each week but the men and women also meet separately at least once a month. Don is the leader of those men's meetings, which typically take place at six o'clock on a weekday morning. Don has a quiet, analytical, and measured personality. He is a student of Scripture and is a spiritually mature believer. Using The Compound Effect Spiritual Maturity Scale to evaluate Don's spiritual maturity, he scored a 6.5 on a scale of 0-10.

As we've discussed, The Compound Effect multiplies the business competency value by the spiritual maturity value to determine the relative value of the individual's Kingdom Impact on a scale of 0-100. In this example, Don's current Kingdom Impact value is 52.7.

The Artist

Andrew is a gifted speaker, writer, and musician. His material is both practical and inspirational. He has a magnetic personality and has spent his entire life absorbing Scripture. He has never been married and devotes himself to worship and prayer at least two hours each day. He serves when asked but has a reputation for getting sidetracked when assignments become tedious, difficult, or too intimate. On The Compound Effect Spiritual Maturity Scale, Andrew falls into the category of a servant and his score is a 6.9.

Andrew has only held two serious jobs in his entire life. He was the artistic and marketing director for a small dot-com company, a position that he was exceptionally well-suited to hold. Unfortunately the company did not survive. However, his work was noticed by a larger, well-known software company and he was offered a position with their marketing department.

Andrew found it very difficult to deal with the structure, the intensity, and the politics that went on within the company. After sixteen months he quit to start his own production company. That was nine years ago. Some of his written material and music has been published locally and he has managed to eek out a living as a music teacher and ski instructor with an occasional stint in construction. When we measured Andrew's business skills and abilities using The Compound Effect Business Competency Scale, his business competence scored a 2.9 on a scale of 0-10. As a result, Andrew's Kingdom Impact factor is 20.01 on a scale of 0-100.

The Pastor

Michael is a dedicated pastor. With his wife and three children, Michael has lived in six different urban communities in eighteen years. His family is highly respected by their denomination and usually gets a call when there is a key congregation in crisis. Michael is a peacemaker, a consensus builder, and a shepherd. His mind is a theological library and his sermons resonate with biblical support, but he shies away from controversial or complex subjects. He is cordial but not friendly, personable but not intimate. His work schedule is highly structured and organized in order to allow maximum time to study and prepare his sermons. On The Compound Effect Spiritual Maturity Scale, Michael scored a 7.0 on a scale of 0-10.

Despite the fact that Michael has served as pastor in six different churches, his largest congregation was one hundred and sixty and his typical Sunday service has sixty or less in attendance. Michael's wife, Anne, handles all of the family's finances and has done so ever since they were married. The family has learned to live a very modest lifestyle, which had the unintended consequence of making budding entrepreneurs out of their two oldest children. Michael Jr. and his younger brother Sean started a lawnmowing service in their early teens, which blossomed into a full-blown landscape company that now holds contracts with several parks and recreation departments to maintain baseball diamonds and soccer fields. The sons now make more money than their father, who marvels at their success.

Their mother has been their coach and mentor.

When we measured Michael's business competence using The Compound Effect Business Competency Scale, he scored a 1.9 out of a possible 10. As a result, after multiplying Michael's Spiritual Maturity by his Business Competence, his relative impact in the kingdom was 13.3. Despite his considerable spiritual maturity, Michael's Kingdom Impact is currently limited to his immediate congregations and the community where he serves.

These three illustrations are characterizations based on true lives and circumstances, although names and minor details have been changed. In a later chapter we will examine some well-documented stories in greater depth, but these examples illustrate how The Compound Effect can help you evaluate your current Kingdom Impact and the areas where you should focus your attention in order to grow and mature in your ability to bring transformation on behalf of God's kingdom during the course of your lifetime. Building Kingdom Impact is a lifetime endeavor and, when done according to God's plans and purposes, will perpetuate and bear fruit for generations to come.

The objective is to encourage you to grow both your business competency and spiritual maturity so you can increase your Kingdom Impact and transform lives now and in the generations to follow. The Compound Effect embraces the idea that your business is your ministry and your ministry is your business. You are only a steward, not an owner, of all the resources at your disposal. Those resources include the time, money, assets, knowledge, and relationships associated with your business. When those resources are deployed with righteousness, wisdom, skill, creativity, and purpose, your Kingdom Impact will be profound.

The stronger your business competency and
the deeper your spiritual maturity,
the greater your Kingdom Impact.

CHAPTER 2

IMPACTING THE WORLD

Do nothing out of selfish ambition
or vain conceit, but in humility
consider others better than yourselves.

— Philippians 2:3

The Bible tells us that God has a plan for our lives. "For I know the plans I have for you, declares the Lord, plans for welfare and not for evil, to give you a future and a hope" (Jeremiah 29:11). We all have a different calling, a particular destiny, a unique purpose. But no matter what our talents, skills, or interests may be, there are five primary tasks that God desires for each one of us to accomplish in our lifetime.

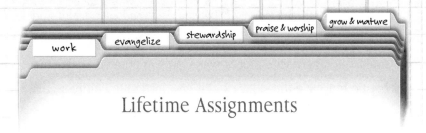

Lifetime Assignments

The first assignment God has for us is to *work*. From the beginning of Creation, God designed mankind to labor and created an economy where man had dominion over the land and sea, plants and animals.

> *Then God said, "Let Us make man in Our image, according to Our likeness; and let them have dominion over the fish of the sea, over the birds of the air, and over the cattle, over all the earth and over every creeping thing that creeps on the earth." So God created man in His own image; in the image of God He created him; male and female He created them. Then God blessed them, and God said to them, "Be fruitful and multiply; and fill the earth, and subdue it; have dominion over*

*the fish of the sea, over the birds of the air, and over
every living thing that moves upon the earth."*

—Genesis 1:26-28

Unfortunately, things changed a bit when Adam and Eve fell. Now work was no longer only a fulfilling purpose, but a necessity for survival. Proverbs says the man who does not work shall not eat. But the good news is God has equipped us to work! In the book of Exodus, we read of Bezalel and Oholiab, who were gifted by God as craftsmen in order to build the tabernacle. Moses was God's appointed leader but he did not have the skills or abilities needed to complete the construction of the tabernacle. Laborers and tradesmen were needed in order to establish the house of the Lord.

The Bible also tells us that all of Jesus' disciples had a vocation and supported themselves when their ministries did not. The apostle Paul—without a doubt the most influential and effective minister of the Christian church— chose to support himself by making tents, rather than relying on his ministry. Regardless of the gifts or talents you may have, whatever your unique niche may be, be assured that God wants you to work!

Make Disciples

Our second assignment is to evangelize. Jesus said,

*Go ye therefore, and make disciples of all the nations,
baptizing them into the name of the Father and of the*

Son and of the Holy Spirit: teaching them to observe
all things whatsoever I commanded you: and lo, I am
with you always, even unto the end of the world.

—Matthew 28:19-20

God's plan is to reach the whole world through men and women who belong to Him. How, when, and where evangelism takes place is our responsibility. God has provided access to salvation through Jesus Christ. He has provided the power to facilitate evangelism through the Holy Spirit. And God has provided the playbook on how to execute evangelism through His Word. Our job is to deliver the message and fulfill the Great Commission.

Effective Stewardship

Our third task is to be good stewards of God's resources. We are charged with investing the time, talents, skills, and assets that He has entrusted to us in such a way that the kingdom of God is expanded and strengthened. Jesus explained this principle in the following parable:

A nobleman went into a far country to receive for
himself a kingdom and then return. Calling ten of his
servants, he gave them ten minas, and said to them,
"Engage in business until I come." But his citizens hated
him and sent a delegation after him, saying, "We do
not want this man to reign over us." When he returned,
having received the kingdom, he ordered these servants

to whom he had given the money to be called to him, that he might know what they had gained by doing business. The first came before him, saying, "Lord, your mina has made ten minas more." And he said to him, "Well done, good servant! Because you have been faithful in a very little, you shall have authority over ten cities." And the second came, saying, "Lord, your mina has made five minas." And he said to him, "And you are to be over five cities." Then another came, saying, "Lord, here is your mina, which I kept laid away in a handkerchief; for I was afraid of you, because you are a severe man. You take what you did not deposit, and reap what you did not sow." He said to him, "I will condemn you with your own words, you wicked servant! You knew that I was a severe man, taking what I did not deposit and reaping what I did not sow? Why then did you not put my money in the bank, and at my coming I might have collected it with interest?" And he said to those who stood by, "Take the mina from him, and give it to the one who has the ten minas." And they said to him, "Lord, he has ten minas!" I tell you that to everyone who has, more will be given, but from the one who has not, even what he has will be taken away.

—Luke 19:12-26

As mature believers, we must come to understand that we are only stewards of the resources at our disposal—not owners. We have the choice to apply His resources with skill and creativity, or waste them. But ultimately God will hold us accountable for our actions and decisions.

A Life of Worship

The fourth critical purpose of our lives is to praise and worship God. "But you are a chosen generation, a royal priesthood, a holy nation, His own special people, that you may proclaim the praises of Him who called you out of darkness into His marvelous light" (1 Peter 2:9). God inhabits our praises. It is during those sincere moments of worship that we are able to come into the presence of God.

True praise and worship acknowledges the power and the might and glory of who He is. True praise and worship offers thanksgiving and appreciation for all the things that the Lord has provided us. True praise and worship acknowledges God as the Creator of all things, without whom we can accomplish nothing.

> We are only stewards of the resources at our disposal —not owners.

What many people do not understand is that real praise and worship is not dependent on our circumstances. It is an act of obedient sacrifice that allows us to open a line of communication with God. And that communication was the primary reason God created us—that He might have relationship with us.

Grow and Mature

Finally, the fifth assignment that God gives us in this life is to grow and mature.

For this very reason, make every effort to add to your faith goodness; and to goodness, knowledge; and to knowledge, self-control; and to self-control, perseverance; and to perseverance, godliness; and to godliness, brotherly kindness; and to brotherly kindness, love. For if you possess these qualities in increasing measure, they will keep you from being ineffective and unproductive in your knowledge of our Lord Jesus Christ.

2 Peter 1:5-8

The key words in this Scripture are "add to" and "increasing measure." The characteristics mentioned in this passage are all necessary to achieve effective results in God's economy. However, we will not be able to develop them, let alone build upon them in increasing measure, unless we are willing to engage in the process of maturing. There is no better insurance policy against an ineffective and unproductive life than maturing in our relationship with God and others.

In nature, all plants and animals go through a maturing process. Our bodies and minds continually grow and change from infancy to adolescence to adulthood, and finally old age. Physical growth and maturity is a natural process. However, spiritual growth and maturity can only be accomplished through the intentional and obedient study of God's Word, continued prayer, and the faithful application of biblical and spiritual principles—through every trial and tribulation, failure and triumph.

Creating Kingdom Impact

We've already learned that we define Kingdom Impact as our ability to transform the lives of the people within our sphere of influence through the application and demonstration of Christ's love and biblical principles. But what does Kingdom Impact look like from God's perspective? What is necessary for legitimate transformation of our world to occur?

The ability to generate Kingdom Impact resides in both individuals and organizations.

The ability to generate Kingdom Impact resides in both individuals and organizations. First, Kingdom Impact transformation requires a life of righteousness through Christ and an adherence to the principles of the Gospels and Scripture. True Kingdom Impact is evidenced by measurable improvements in the physical, spiritual, social, and financial existence of people. True transformation also implies that these changes are positive and sustained through multiple generations, demonstrating an overall improvement in quality of life, physical well-being, social harmony, and political freedom.

Only Kingdom Impact contains the power to bring about this kind of sustainable transformation. We can harness this power by recognizing our rights and responsibilities as followers of Christ, by applying biblical principles to our human interactions and relationships, and by applying the resources that God has entrusted to us—including time, knowledge, relationships, creativity, finances, and possessions.

When God's power is applied with honor, humility, and integrity, sustainable transformation will result. When God's power is misappropriated, families, communities, and nations are destroyed and generational curses are created. How do we obtain the power required to achieve sustainable Kingdom Impact? How do we obtain the ability to transform lives? How do we apply this transformational power exponentially?

We must accumulate wisdom—otherwise known as competence.

Wisdom is supreme; therefore get wisdom. Though it cost all you have, get understanding.

—Proverbs 4:7

We must accumulate knowledge.

Teach me knowledge and good judgment, for I believe in your commands.

—Psalm 119:66

We must accumulate experience.

Look, I have grown and increased in wisdom more than anyone who has ruled over Jerusalem before me; I have experienced much of wisdom and knowledge.

—Ecclesiastes 1:16

We must distribute resources appropriately.

Honor the LORD with your wealth, with the firstfruits of all your crops.

—Proverbs 3:9

We must build and store resources consistently.

Then your barns will be filled to overflowing, and your vats will brim over with new wine.

—Proverbs 3:10

We must seek God for direction.

Trust in the LORD with all your heart and lean not on your own understanding.

—Proverbs 3:5

We must plan and prepare carefully.

I also said to him, "If it pleases the king, may I have letters to the governors of Trans-Euphrates, so that they will provide me safe-conduct until I arrive in Judah? And may I have a letter to Asaph, keeper of the king's forest, so he will give me timber to make beams for the gates of the citadel by the temple and for the city wall and for the residence I will occupy?" And because the gracious hand of my God was upon me, the king granted my requests. So I went to the

*governors of Trans-Euphrates and gave them the
king's letters. The king had also sent army officers
and cavalry with me.*

—Nehemiah 2:7-9

We must skillfully recognize and gauge adversity.

*Hear us, O our God, for we are despised. Turn their
insults back on their own heads. Give them over as
plunder in a land of captivity. Do not cover up their
guilt or blot out their sins from your sight, for they
have thrown insults in the face of the builders.*

—Nehemiah 4:4-5

We must plan and execute with diligence and discipline.

*Above all else, guard your heart, for it is the well-
spring of life.*

*Put away perversity from your mouth; keep corrupt
talk far from your lips.*

*Let your eyes look straight ahead, fix your gaze directly
before you.*

*Make level paths for your feet and take only ways that
are firm.*

*Do not swerve to the right or the left; keep your foot
from evil.*

—Proverbs 4:23-27

We must serve others with integrity.

*I put in charge of Jerusalem my brother Hanani,
along with Hananiah the commander of the citadel,
because he was a man of integrity and feared God*

more than most men do.

—Nehemiah 7:2

We must remain humble and content.

Do nothing out of selfish ambition or vain conceit, but in humility consider others better than yourselves.

—Philippians 2:3

The books of Proverbs and Nehemiah are a veritable business instruction manual on how to apply God's power and use your business resources for sustainable Kingdom Impact. These Scriptures outline in great detail how to solve problems and engage with people God's way. Nehemiah made decisions and choices, but God directed his steps.

What happens when sustainable Kingdom Impact occurs? What is the result when God's power is manifested through you?

◆ God's plans and purposes are fulfilled.

◆ God is recognized as the ultimate resource.

◆ Lives are transformed.

◆ Nations are restored and built.

◆ People serve one another.

◆ Resources are multiplied.

◆ Poverty, disease, despair, and tyranny are replaced with prosperity, health, hope, and freedom.

The Challenging Reality

So how do we expand the influence—the Kingdom Impact—of the Christian business community? One answer is launching new businesses that are built and operated according to biblical principles and reflect Christ in the marketplace.

The reality is that starting a business of any kind today is a significant challenge. There are a number of significant hurdles to overcome:

◆ Business models that worked fifteen to twenty years ago, are no longer effective today. They are obsolete. New operating models are emerging that are untried and unproven. Nevertheless, many will succeed.

◆ There is a profound tension between the necessity of earning a living to feed one's family and the sacrifices necessary to establish a truly successful self-sustaining business that has positive Kingdom Impact. The risks are considerable.

◆ The financial capital required to launch and sustain a new business and reach profitability is larger today than it has ever been.

◆ Our rapidly changing technology and global economy can render a profitable business obsolete overnight.

◆ Trying to determine how to deploy resources in today's rapidly changing political climate offers as great an opportunity for failure as it does for success.

◆ Building a significant, sustainable business still

requires a minimum of twenty years and, in most
cases, at least fifty years—or two generations, before
it can reach the point that it has material Kingdom
Impact. There are some exceptions to this reality,
but they are very rare and usually not sustainable.

The idea of putting one's family at risk for the purpose
of launching a new business is a choice not generally understood or supported by most churches or pastors. I experienced this firsthand when, at the age of twenty-six and with
two children under the age of three, my wife and I decided
to launch a new business with a $5,000 loan from a friend.
We had incredible support from the business community
and received coaching and direction from several local business owners. Our business became profitable within eighteen months. During that period in our lives we were active
within the church and tithed consistently from our earnings.
But it never even crossed our minds that we should seek
spiritual support from our pastor, and he never offered.

The local church has seldom embraced the idea that young
people should prayerfully devote themselves to acquiring the
skills and abilities required to build a thriving, profitable,
kingdom-minded business. Interestingly enough, churches
and pastors consistently encourage young families to put
their security at risk by sacrificing to serve in the mission field
or the ministry, but seldom do they encourage or promote
entrepreneurship as an acceptable Christian lifestyle.

In fact, given that 98 percent of all young people

will find careers in the secular marketplace and not in the ministry, shouldn't our churches play a larger role in preparing individuals to serve Christ in the marketplace? The current lack of encouragement and support for young entrepreneurs might be one explanation as to why the majority of young people today are not attracted to getting involved in a local church. The truth is that local churches who are not responsive to current marketplace realities risk becoming irrelevant.

It is critical that our churches begin to embrace the unique challenges and callings on our Christian business leaders.

If we are truly going to have Kingdom Impact through the influence and strength of our businesses, it is critical that our churches begin to embrace the unique challenges and callings on our Christian business leaders. What better purpose can we find for ministry leadership to encourage, train, and support Christian-owned businesses as they grow and prosper, than advancing the kingdom of God?

Profitable, thriving God-centered businesses have been the financial backbone of ministries and missions for the past two thousand years. In the Old Testament, the Levites were supported by tithes from merchants, farmers, and tradesmen. Churches today need to recognize the value of the business owners within their congregations—not just for their financial resources, but also for their influence in the lives of those they serve. Believers, pastors, ministries, and churches need to learn how to support and encourage entrepreneurship.

Plugging into the Source

I live in Colorado Springs and every morning when I look out my window, I am awed by the majesty of Pikes Peak, which dominates our skyline with its presence and splendor. Its appearance changes by the hour, by the day, and by the season. There are many facets to the mountain, and they all play a role in its makeup—the snowcapped peak, the barren, rugged rock, the distinctive silhouette, the shrouded monster that spews lightning, thunder, and howling rain.

Adventurous climbers can ascend the mountain, but only at certain times and even then, only with careful planning and appropriate preparation. There are some who scale its trails regularly and consider it a close friend. There are many who could never climb it, nor would they ever dream of trying. Even the drive to the top can be a treacherous experience. Yet, despite its many varied characteristics, it is the same mountain and in the end it doesn't change its height, its dimension, or its presence.

Pikes Peak is a reflection and reminder of God's power. It defines our city. No man put it there and no man will remove it. It reminds me how limited and finite I am in the context of God's omnipotent power. If we can begin to understand His power, we can tap into its source and learn to apply it to transform lives and expand His kingdom through our businesses and ministries.

Like swimming with the current in an ocean or a mighty river, we must learn to harness God's power by recognizing His requirements, His expectations, His resources, and His methods. God's methods always start in the spiritual realm, but become evident through the physical and natural. He has the power to accomplish whatever He desires and already has a plan in place to do so. God's purpose is to accomplish His plans through the application of our gifts, talents, and abilities. Each of us has a choice to participate in His plan. We can choose to be part of the problem or part of His solution.

God's power is infinite. His power is beyond measure. But is this power available to you and me? Absolutely! His limitless power is available through a personal relationship with Jesus Christ. The Bible says,

> *That if you confess with your mouth, 'Jesus is Lord,' and believe in your heart that God raised him from the dead, you will be saved. For it is with your heart that you believe and are justified, and it is with your mouth that you confess and are saved.*
> —Romans 10:9-10

A personal relationship with Jesus Christ is available to every person through grace, which is defined as "unmerited favor." Salvation is something we do not deserve and cannot earn. I gave my heart to Jesus more than forty years ago. He has walked beside me ever since, despite my many bad decisions and negative attitudes. Today I am blessed beyond measure. You cannot do anything to receive salvation other than believe in your heart that Jesus Christ is the Son of God. Such a simple, yet powerful choice. Your decision to accept Christ will become the turning point in your life, regardless of where you find yourself today.

CHAPTER 3

THE POWER OF A SEED

Others, like seed sown on good soil,
hear the word, accept it, and produce
a crop—thirty, sixty, or even
a hundred times what was sown.

— Mark 4:20

If we look at the natural order of things, it is very evident that God demonstrates His creative power and divine wisdom through the process of multiplication. The Scriptures often talk about seeds, which are the ultimate example of multiplication in nature. A single seed of wheat produces a new plant with a head of wheat that contains between eighty and two hundred and fifty seed kernels. A single apple seed may grow into an apple tree that produces hundreds of thousands of apples over its lifetime. A single olive seed may be propagated into an entire orchard that may stand through multiple generations.

Of course, certain conditions must be met for multiplication to be possible. First, a seed must be planted in good soil. This must be followed by proper cultivation, patience, perseverance, and preparation for the harvest. Any skilled farmer or gardener will tell you that preparation of the soil is the critical first step to growing a bountiful crop. There are other key factors that can affect a crop, including appropriate soil temperature for germination, moisture for sustained growth, nutrients to encourage maximum yield, and protection from adversaries such as insects, fungus, weeds, and unpredictable weather. When the fruit is ripe it must be quickly and efficiently harvested at exactly the right time and taken to storage or to market. Planting the seed is only the beginning.

Good friends of mine operate an eleven thousand-acre

Kansas dryland wheat farm that has been in their family for more than fifty years. Some years they have seen bumper crops, while other years have produced absolutely no crop at all. The price of wheat has been as low as $1 per bushel, and as high as $9 per bushel. The improvements in the technology and sophistication of farm equipment enables five men to farm eleven thousand acres. Fifty years ago, farming those eleven thousand acres would have taken at

least thirty men. But over the course of more than fifty seasons of planting and harvesting, that land has yielded in excess of fifteen million bushels of wheat. This is the power of multiplication in action, according to God's plan and purpose.

Seeds in the Heart

So how does God's power become multiplied for the purpose of improving the human condition? The first and primary prerequisite is prayer. God's power cannot be appropriated through our lives unless there is regular communication with Him. Fortunately, the Bible provides ample demonstration and direction on what to pray, how to pray, and when to pray. Praise and worship is also a key component. The Bible tells us that God inhabits our praises. And what many people do not realize is that prayer also requires *listening* to what God has to say on the subject or need placed before Him. Both the Old and

New Testament are full of examples of prayers that God answered—often with a response that was not what was requested or expected.

Abraham was appointed by God to be the father of nations—despite being beyond the age of childbearing. Joseph was chosen and trained through difficult circumstances to become God's emissary within a heathen culture. David, despite all his weaknesses and shortcomings, was favored by God and entrusted with the protection of a nation. It is interesting that almost every biblical personality that God selected to demonstrate and promote His will came from the marketplace. Abraham was a businessman. Jesus was a carpenter. David was a shepherd. Nehemiah was a servant in the king's court. Peter was a fisherman. Luke was a doctor. Paul was a tax collector and became a tentmaker to support his ministry.

Today, there are countless men and women around the world serving at God's direction in one or more of the five-fold ministries. Most of these men and women serve in and through the marketplace. This is the human resources aspect of God's economy. He is actively seeking recruits with not only the right heart, but also the willingness to serve and sacrifice everything to accomplish His will.

The Bible clearly defines the types of character traits that we need to possess in order to be entrusted with God's multiplying power. The key is that those characteristics are quite different from those of a person who is operating in his own power and leveraging his human capabilities and understanding. We are stewards of God's resources, time, assets, finances, creativity, and relationships. Biblical stewardship is the process of multiplying those resources to serve and expand God's kingdom on earth.

It has always been God's plan to accomplish His will through people—for that is how His power is most effectively multiplied and demonstrated. His plan for the redemption and salvation of mankind was fulfilled through His Son, Jesus Christ. But God's strategy involved Jesus spending three and a half years teaching, coaching, and training twelve disciples who would be charged with the task of delivering and demonstrating the gospel to the world. It took those disciples the rest of their lives to fully achieve their appointed tasks, but the transformation that God achieved through those men was remarkable in its scope and influence. The result of twelve seeds planted and the power of multiplication at work!

Ministry in the Marketplace

For many people, there is a big distinction between business and ministry. They see church on Sunday as being "true" ministry, while the business of the marketplace is just a necessity of life, to be conducted from Monday through Saturday, until they can get back to "ministering." A typical local church will make contact with the majority of its members once a week. Now consider that for every church, there are more than one hundred businesses. For every single church employee, there are more than 150 employees in the marketplace.

A wonderful book, *Anointed for Business* by Ed Silvoso, changed my personal paradigm. For the first time, my eyes were opened to the reality that as a man called to the business world, my business was my ministry. I was astounded to realize that real ministry did not revolve solely around the pulpit and church meetings on Sunday.

> For every single church employee, there are more than 150 employees in the marketplace.

Jesus spent the first thirty years of his life as part of a working class family and learning a trade. He spent three and a half years in ministry. It is no coincidence that virtually all of His ministry took place where the people were—in the markets and streets of cities and villages.

By virtue of the relationships I had established through my business, I was already in ministry seven days a week and did not need to go to the mission field or become a pastor to bring about Kingdom Impact. My mission field was all around me every day—starting in my home with my own family.

Along with this paradigm shift came the additional understanding that my business was not only my ministry, but it was also the core of my testimony. How I operated my business and treated customers, employees, vendors, and suppliers was a direct reflection on my relationship with Jesus. My attitudes and actions, as well as the operations and profitability of my business either expanded or detracted from the kingdom of God.

Looking Inward

Certainly there are those who are called into traditional full-time ministry. But if you are like most believers, you will primarily serve God in a different capacity—using whatever gifts and abilities He has given you as you go about your daily responsibilities. In order to understand the principles of The Compound Effect and be able to measure and evaluate our progress, we need to take an honest look at our lives. Take some time and ask yourself the following questions:

1. Do I have a life plan?

2. What are my current God-given gifts, talents, abilities, and skills?

3. What is God's lifetime assignment for me?

4. Do I have the depth of faith required to allow the Lord to be in charge of my life's assignment?

5. How is God preparing me for my lifetime assignment?

6. What valuable lifetime experiences do I have that can be applied by the Lord in a business setting?

7. Does my life plan include participating in and contributing to sustainable kingdom transformation of the lives of all the people with whom I interact daily?

8. Is my life plan self-centered, other-centered, or Christ-centered?

9. Where am I today in terms of my spiritual maturity and business competency? Am I an infant, adolescent, adult, or a seasoned citizen in these two areas?

10. How has the level of my spiritual maturity and business competency affected the level of my sustainable Kingdom Impact to this point?

11. Do I have the social and organizational skills required to steward and manage the resources that God has entrusted to me?

12. What skills, talents, and abilities do I need to continue to develop in order to be entrusted by God with greater responsibilities?

13. Do I fully and completely understand God's plan for the multiplication of His power?

14. Do I have the moral character and appropriate levels of humility and obedience to be entrusted with transformation responsibilities and Kingdom Impact power?

15. Am I fully prepared to engage the faith required to put God's multiplication power into action?

16. What level of sustainable Kingdom Impact, kingdom influence, and kingdom transformation can God accomplish through me in the course of my lifetime?

17. Who has the bigger vision for my life, God or me?

18. What is my vehicle for sustainable kingdom transformation?

19. To what specific area has God assigned me? Is it business, ministry, government, education, the arts, or media?

These are not easy questions to answer—and some answers you may not like. A few may take a lifetime to be revealed. Arriving at a valid evaluation will require the study of Scripture, prayer, realistic self-assessment, journaling, engaging wise counsel, and hard work. But if you are serious about making your business your ministry and maximizing your Kingdom Impact, it is important that you continue to honestly address these questions as we continue to study the principles of The Compound Effect.

CHAPTER 4

THE ROAD TO SPIRITUAL MATURITY

Perseverance must finish its work
so that you may be mature and complete,
not lacking anything.

— James 1:4

All living things grow and mature—if not, to put it simply, they are no longer living. In the same way, experiencing continued spiritual growth is part of the natural process of living a life in Christ. Jesus said, "Abide in Me, and I in you. As the branch cannot bear fruit of itself unless it abides in the vine, so neither can you unless you abide in Me. I am the vine, you are the branches; he who abides in Me and I in him, he bears much fruit, for apart from Me you can do nothing" (John 15:4-5). If we want to grow and bear mature, plentiful fruit, we must abide in Him.

We have already read 2 Peter 1:5-9, which describes the specific behaviors that are our desired "fruit": faith, goodness, knowledge, self-control, perseverance, godliness, brotherly kindness, and love. It is not enough to simply apply a small amount of these specific characteristics—we must increase in them in order to become mature in our relationship with Jesus Christ. If we do not grow—continually improving and maturing—we will become ineffective and unproductive in our lives, our witness to others, and our service to God.

If we do not grow we will become ineffective and unproductive.

Measuring Maturity

So how do we know whether we are growing and maturing? The challenge is that spiritual growth and maturity is intangible. There are no outward physical features that can be measured to determine how much growth is actually taking place. However, spiritual growth and maturity can be gauged within the context of our behaviors.

The Weavers Scale of Spiritual Growth and Maturity was developed for this very purpose. This important tool measures growth by defining specific behaviors that characterize different levels of spiritual maturity, and then assigns a relative value to that behavior. For example, our seasons of life—infancy, childhood, adolescence, and adulthood—are all characterized and measured in the context of certain milestones. Most frequently, they are measured in the numerical values of days, weeks, months, and years. Would it not be logical for our spiritual maturity to also follow a logical progression? And if our physical growth can be measured, why not our spiritual growth?

The Weavers Scale was designed as a tool to be used to evaluate an individual's spiritual condition at any given time. It should not be used as a comparative device to place believers in competition with one another for spiritual supremacy. When you first complete the Weavers Scale, the initial assessment should establish a benchmark for your current level of spiritual maturity and reveal specific behaviors that might need to be addressed.

You can then use The Weavers Scale periodically to assess any changes and growth that has taken place.

Subsequent results should reveal improvements in behavior, attitude, and knowledge. This tool will help you identify where to focus your efforts in order to improve current behaviors and develop greater levels of spiritual maturity.

At a meeting not long ago, I was teaching the concept of spiritual growth and maturity to seventy men when I asked the following questions:

How many of you read the Bible daily?

How many of you memorize Scripture on a regular basis?

How many of you are lifetime students of Scripture?

By the time I had reached the third question, less than 5 percent of the hands in the room were raised. These were all spiritually mature men, most of whom were forty years old or older. They were all active members of a men's fellowship group that met for two hours every week to pray, study the Word, and fellowship.

This group of men was exceptionally mature in comparison to any similar demographic. But the sad reality is that only a very small percentage of Christians ever actually read the Bible, let alone memorize or study the depth of its meaning. This is particularly unfortunate because the Bible is full of passages that support and encourage spiritual growth and maturity in our lives. God gave us everything we need to know to transform the world, but very few believers are studying the instruction manual.

Therefore let us go on and get past the elementary stage in the teachings and doctrine of Christ (the Messiah), advancing steadily toward the completeness and perfection that belong to spiritual maturity. Let us not again be laying the foundation of repentance and abandonment of dead works (dead formalism) and of the faith [by which you turned] to God, with teachings about purifying, the laying on of hands, the resurrection from the dead, and eternal judgment and punishment. [These are all matters of which you should have been fully aware long, long ago.] If indeed God permits, we will [now] proceed [to advanced teaching].

—Hebrews 6:1-3

That we may present every person mature (full-grown, fully initiated, complete, and perfect) in Christ (the Anointed One).

—Colossians 1:28

Until we all reach unity in the faith and in the knowledge of the Son of God and become mature, attaining to the whole measure of the fullness of Christ. Then we will no longer be infants, tossed back and forth by the waves, and blown here and there by every wind of teaching and by the cunning and craftiness of men in their deceitful scheming.

—Ephesians 4:13-14

Not that I have already obtained all this, or have already been made perfect, but I press on to take

hold of that for which Christ Jesus took hold of me.
Brothers, I do not consider myself yet to have taken
hold of it. But one thing I do: Forgetting what is
behind and straining toward what is ahead, I press
on toward the goal to win the prize for which God has
called me heavenward in Christ Jesus. All of us who
are mature should take such a view of things.

—Philippians 3:12-15

But solid food is for the mature, who by constant use
have trained themselves to distinguish good from evil.

—Hebrews 5:14

A Gradual Progression

Consider this—as an eighteen-month-old child, you were not yet ready to operate an automobile. Similarly, God's power will not be made available to you if you are not mature enough to understand how to apply it for His glory and service. Spiritual maturity and business competency are alike in that they can only be developed through seasons of testing and experience. Over time you will develop spiritual discernment and wisdom, as well as business competencies and skills that the Lord can use to advance His kingdom. The following

Spiritual maturity and business competency are alike in that they can only be developed through seasons of testing and experience.

analogy compares the maturing seasons of a natural life to the growth and maturing in the life of a business.

1. **Infancy** – The characteristics of infancy are survival and dependence. Any business starting from scratch is in the survival mode for up to five years.

2. **Childhood** – This phase of a business is characterized by learning and increasing independence. At this point the future of the business is no longer seriously in doubt.

3. **Preteen** – In this phase of development, a business goes through the process of learning and discovery. The business is trying to figure out who they really are.

4. **Adolescence** – A business goes through its teenage years and is still learning but is now taking on social and civil responsibility.

5. **Young Adult** – A business is now learning how to apply everything it has learned in the past eighteen years. It is also now ready to take advantage of institutions of higher learning and adopt more sophisticated and complex systems, processes, products, and services.

6. **Adult** – Once a business reaches twenty- to twenty-five years of age, it is now a parent or leader, is fully committed to a life plan and destination, and has the necessary wisdom and

resources to execute that plan.

7. **Senior** – A business that is around fifty or sixty years old now takes on the posture of a grandparent with extensive influence and respect in the community and the world.

It is fairly unusual for an infant, child, or adolescent to have any positive long-term impact in their community, their nation, or the world. In the same way, it is unrealistic to expect a new believer or an emerging business to have a profound Kingdom Impact. During your first years as a Christian business owner, you should be "raising the child" and focused on establishing a competent, prosperous, profitable business that serves your customers and demonstrates biblical principles in the operation of that business. The process of developing spiritual maturity in your life is no different. It requires time and growth to reach a level where you can begin to manifest significant Kingdom Impact.

CHAPTER 5

THE USER, THE SERVANT, THE LEADER

Teach me knowledge and good judgment, for I
believe in your commands.

— Psalm 119:66

I n the first chapter, we talked briefly about the three types of behaviors that define the characteristics of a Christian's spiritual maturity—the **user**, the **servant**, and the **leader**.

◆ The basic believer, otherwise known as the **user**, is defined by the statement, *"It's about me and Jesus."*

◆ The committed believer, otherwise known as the **servant**, is defined by the state-ment, *"It's about you and Jesus."*

◆ The transforming believer, oth-erwise known as the **leader**, is defined by the statement, *"It's about Jesus and His kingdom."*

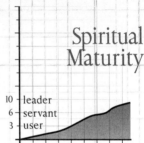

Several months ago I had an opportunity to speak to a men's group. I had been asked to present the topic of spiritual growth and maturity and help this group of men participate in the Weavers Scale assessment. About two o'clock, the morning before the presentation, the Lord woke me up—as He often does when He has something important to tell me.

As I lay there praying about my presentation, God planted a picture in my head of me driving my car, while He was the passenger sitting in the seat next to me. I was driving, He was along for the ride. I was behaving like a user—I was in charge.

Then God showed me a second picture. Again, I was

driving down the road in my car and He was in the passenger seat. However, this time He had a map and was navigating. He was deciding when and where we should turn, but I still was in control of the wheel. The territory was familiar and most of the time I knew where we were and felt very safe. I was listening to God and paying close attention to His direction and behaving as a servant—I was doing what He told me to do.

Finally, God showed me a third picture. I was in my car, but this time God was driving and I was the passenger. The first sensation I had was that the ride was incredibly smooth. There seemed to be fewer bumps, however, the scenery was completely foreign and I had no idea where we were going. Every turn opened up a new panorama of opportunity. I was going places I never dreamed of, seeing things I could have never imagined, and accomplishing things I would have never believed were possible. I was behaving as a leader and letting God drive my car; God was in charge and I was along for the ride.

I demonstrated this to the men at the meeting that morning by putting two chairs side-by-side. First, I took the left seat and the seat on my right was occupied by God. I pretended to drive, but with some degree of regularity managed to run into something with a thump.

Then I explained that I needed help navigating and asked God to navigate for me. We seemed to bump into fewer things. The ride was definitely smoother. Then I got out of the left seat, moved over to the right seat, and allowed God to drive. I was now a leader, relying entirely on God to direct and protect me.

The **user** drives the car and allows God to ride along. The **servant** drives the car and asks God for directions. But the **leader** allows God to drive the car wherever He desires and watches the scenery with anticipation and excitement for what lies around the corner.

The Process of Change

Many of us struggle with the concepts of spiritual growth and maturity. What does it look like? How does it feel? What should we do or not do? How do we know if we are maturing? When trying to answer this type of question, the best source for answers is the Bible. Can you think of a key Bible character who went through a documented maturing process? What did that look like? How did he or she do it?

There are countless excellent examples in Scripture, but the concept of measured spiritual growth and maturity was clearly demonstrated through the life of Peter. We are first introduced to Peter in the Gospels. He was one of the first disciples selected by Jesus. He was a fisherman by trade; a large, boisterous man by description; passionate in his beliefs; and loyal to his commitments. And during the course of his life Peter clearly transitioned from a **user** to a **servant** to a **leader**.

As Jesus was walking beside the Sea of Galilee, he saw two brothers, Simon called Peter and his brother

*Andrew. They were casting a net into the lake, for
they were fishermen. "Come, follow me," Jesus said,
"and I will make you fishers of men." At once they left
their nets and followed him.*

—Matthew 4:18-20

Over the next three and a half years, Jesus coached
and trained Peter and the other eleven disciples to understand their roles and responsibilities, exposing them to the
power of God, and revealing the tasks they would have to
undertake to transform the world.

Our first indication of Peter's incredible faith in Jesus
comes when he miraculously walks on the water.

*During the fourth watch of the night Jesus went out
to them, walking on the lake. When the disciples saw
him walking on the lake, they were terrified. "It's
a ghost," they said, and cried out in fear. But Jesus
immediately said to them: "Take courage! It is I. Don't
be afraid."*

*"Lord, if it's you," Peter replied, "tell me to come to
you on the water."*

"Come," he said.

*Then Peter got down out of the boat, walked on the
water and came toward Jesus.*

—Matthew 14:25-29

In that moment, Peter demonstrated a great capacity for trust and obedience. However, as soon as he came to the realization that he might be in personal danger, Peter began to sink and Jesus had to rescue him. This is our first indication that Peter is operating in the **user** mode. He is still concerned for himself. He is still trying to do things in his own power and ultimately fails.

A short time later Jesus asks His disciples:

"Who do people say the Son of Man is?"
They replied, "Some say John the Baptist; others say Elijah; and still others, Jeremiah or one of the prophets."
"But what about you?" he asked. "Who do you say I am?"
Simon Peter answered, "You are the Christ, the Son of the living God."
Jesus replied, "Blessed are you, Simon son of Jonah, for this was not revealed to you by man, but by my Father in heaven. And I tell you that you are Peter, and on this rock I will build my church, and the gates of Hades will not overcome it. I will give you the keys of the kingdom of heaven; whatever you bind on earth will be bound in heaven, and whatever you loose on earth will be loosed in heaven."

—Matthew 16:13-19

In this one sentence Peter was given an incredible charge. Christ has just given him the keys to the kingdom. However, Peter is not yet spiritually mature enough to completely understand what is at stake. His spirit comprehends but his mind has not yet caught up. Peter is still in the **user** mode.

How many times have we received a vision or an idea that we did not truly comprehend when it arrived? How often have we had an encounter or an event that was seemingly unrelated to anything else in our experience? How many of us have accumulated a vast wealth of knowledge and experience only to find that how we eventually applied it was not at all what we originally set out to do? God's plans for us are usually broader and wider and higher than any of us can possibly imagine. So it was with Peter. However, it took his entire lifetime to accomplish the task the Lord gave him—that of being the rock upon which the church was built.

> God's plans for us are usually broader and wider and higher than any of us can possibly imagine.

Growing Pains

As time went on, all of the disciples, including Peter, watched Jesus perform an array of miracles and observed Him ministering to tens of thousands of people. They witnessed His compassion, love, wisdom, and wrath. They also observed His power. However, none of them, including Peter, fully understood that they, too, would eventually have access to that same power.

Despite all the time they spent with Jesus, the disciples still wanted to know, "What's in it for me?" Jesus told them, "I tell you the truth, it is hard for a rich man to enter the kingdom of heaven. Again I tell you, it is easier for a camel to go through the eye of a needle than for a rich man to enter the kingdom of God" (Matthew 19:23-24). When the disciples heard this, they were greatly astonished and asked how anyone could possibly be saved. Jesus answered, "With man this is impossible, but with God all things are possible" (Matthew 19:26). Then Peter reveals the state of his level of maturity when he says, "We have left everything to follow you! What then will there be for us?" (Matthew 19:27). Obviously, Peter is still in the **user** mode.

We learn from reading further in the Scriptures that Jesus was disappointed, but not surprised that His disciples were continuing to operate in the user mode. At the Last Supper He predicted not only His betrayal at the hands of Judas, but also that Peter would deny Him three times before the sun came up. Peter adamantly rejected the idea and declared that he would die before he would ever deny Jesus. The other disciples expressed the same conviction.

But after Jesus was taken away and Peter was confronted about his association with Jesus, he denied his Lord as was predicted.

Peter replied, 'Man, I don't know what you're talk-ing about!' Just as he was speaking, the rooster

crowed. The Lord turned and looked straight at
Peter. Then Peter remembered the word the Lord
had spoken to him: 'Before the rooster crows today,
you will disown me three times.' And he went out-
side and wept bitterly.

—Luke 22:60-62

Peter wept because he had come to the realization that he was still a user. He had put himself before Christ. This is a difficult lesson for us to learn. If we were to be completely honest, most of us would admit that we live in the user mode. Despite the fact that we have been given incredible gifts, talents, skills, abilities, and experiences, when circumstances become really challenging we are still more concerned about ourselves. When push comes to shove, we will put ourselves before Jesus most of the time.

But the good news is that Peter did not stay there. The growth process that he was going through was part of God's plan. The crucifixion and resurrection of Christ laid the foundation for Peter and the remaining ten disciples to mature into the **servant** mode, eventually developing into the leaders Jesus had trained them to be.

After His resurrection, Jesus appeared to His disciples and used that time to continue the process of training and preparation for their roles as ministers of the gospel of salvation. Jesus said,

This is what I told you while I was still with you:

Everything must be fulfilled that is written about me in the Law of Moses, the Prophets and the Psalms."
Then Jesus opened their minds so they could understand the Scriptures and said, "This is what is written: The Christ will suffer and rise from the dead on the third day, and repentance and forgiveness of sins will be preached in his name to all nations, beginning at Jerusalem. You are witnesses of these things. I am going to send you what my Father has promised; but stay in the city until you have been clothed with power from on high.

—Luke 24:43-49

After all that had happened, Jesus was making the final preparations for His disciples to begin operating in the **servant** and **leader** modes.

New Levels of Maturity

Peter's transition from the **user** mode to the **servant** and **leader** modes is recorded for us in the book of Acts. Following Jesus' ascension, the disciples and their followers are sequestered in a small building in Jerusalem. On the day of Pentecost, a mighty wind came through the room, filling everyone present with the power of the Holy Spirit. After this transformational event, Peter is the first one to speak and address the group.

Then Peter stood up with the Eleven, raised his voice

and addressed the crowd: "Fellow Jews and all of you who live in Jerusalem, let me explain this to you; listen carefully to what I say. These men are not drunk, as you suppose. It's only nine in the morning! No, this is what was spoken by the prophet Joel:

"'In the last days, God says, I will pour out my Spirit on all people. Your sons and daughters will prophesy, your young men will see visions, your old men will dream dreams. Even on my servants, both men and women, I will pour out my Spirit in those days, and they will prophesy. I will show wonders in the heaven above and signs on the earth below, blood and fire and billows of smoke. The sun will be turned to darkness and the moon to blood before the coming of the great and glorious day of the Lord. And everyone who calls on the name of the Lord will be saved.'"

—Acts 2:14-21

At this point, we can see clear evidence that Peter is now in the servant mode and well on his way to becoming recognized as a leader. During the next several chapters of Acts we learn that Peter heals a crippled beggar, speaks to crowds, is seized by the Sanhedrin, and brought before them to be questioned about the miracles he is performing in the name of Jesus. "When they saw the courage of Peter and John and realized that they were unschooled, ordinary men, they were astonished and they took note that these men had been with Jesus" (Acts 4:13).

But there were still lessons to be learned and adjustments to be made. Later on in the book of Acts, an angel appeared to Peter in a dream. God wanted to challenge the common belief that was concealed in Peter's heart—that the Gentiles were inferior and not worthy of the gospel of Jesus Christ. Eventually, as Peter allowed God to deal with his heart, he became a critical link to fulfill God's plan to spread the gospel among the Gentile peoples. Peter continued to grow and mature, through the help of the Holy Spirit.

We learn more about Peter's life as we read the books of first and second Peter. These missives that Peter wrote provide clear evidence that Peter was finally operating as a leader—the one that Jesus described when He said, "Upon this rock I will build my church; and the gates of hell shall not prevail against it" (Matthew 16:18). Peter displays his leadership by giving specific direction to the church for living as Christians. Peter leaves a legacy of instruction on holy living, submission to authority, marriage, suffering, eldership, desirable behavior, prophecy, and false teaching.

Men and women who possess great spiritual maturity leave long-lasting legacies. But everyone begins at the same place—lost and in desperate need of God. Peter began his growth process in the marketplace as a fisherman—a man with business competence, but very little spiritual maturity. Then, on a fateful, God-ordained day, he was chosen, just as he was, to be loved, mentored, and trained by Jesus. It was only through the experiences and challenges of following Jesus during His ministry, then carrying on after the Crucifixion, and finally moving forward through the power of the Holy Spirit, that he ceased being a user and began to operate in the leader's role Christ had prepared for him. Once Peter understood and accepted his role as the foundation of the church, he fully matured and became one of the most powerful spiritual leaders to ever walk the face of the earth—fulfilling his God-given destiny. God desires the same outcome for each one of us today.

CHAPTER 6

THE WEAVERS SCALE ASSESSMENT

The crucible for silver and the furnace for gold,
but the LORD tests the heart.

— Proverbs 17:3

Some might say that measuring spiritual growth and maturity is inappropriate or too subjective to be relevant. Others might argue that it's a dangerous exercise because it might lend itself to pride and distorted self-importance. These outcomes are all possible. Nevertheless, the potential benefits derived from a tool that can help each of us evaluate our spiritual growth and maturity far outweigh the possible drawbacks.

Having said that, it must be understood that the following tool can only be relevant and properly applied through continual study of the Word, worship, and prayer. For each topic, you will find specific Scriptures that are intended to help you gain further understanding for how to improve your behavior in that area.

I believe that if you will honestly evaluate your heart in regard to each of the following subjects, you will gain an accurate picture of the condition of your life and your level of spiritual maturity. (For a summary of these priciples see Table 6.1 on page 111.)

SALVATION

The **user** *has been through the salvation experience.*

The **servant** *models and promotes the salvation experience.*

The **leader** *maintains an intimate relationship with Father, Son, and Holy Spirit.*

Users have had a sincere salvation experience. They understand that a significant event has occurred in their lives, bringing them into a personal relationship with Jesus Christ. Something is different. They sense a presence that was not evident prior to salvation. They have had a change of heart. They are not sure what it means yet, but they know that it is real.

Servants begin to walk out their salvation according to biblical truths. They are students of Scripture. Their behavior begins to change. They think and act differently and actively seek to understand what their relationship with Christ means in the context of their day-to-day living. They begin to study the Bible in order to seek answers to their questions about life. They engage with and actively reach out to serve others.

Leaders promote and encourage salvation as the solution to life's challenges. They teach and model biblical truths in their own lives. To those who are unsaved, leaders communicate salvation as a gift that cannot be earned or deserved, but is available through grace and the power of God. They demonstrate the path to holiness, purity, righteousness, and sacrifice through a life in Christ. Leaders attract others and encourage them to grow and mature in their walk with the Lord.

They replied, "Believe in the Lord Jesus, and you will be saved—you and your household."
—Acts 16:31

Jesus said to the woman, "Your faith has saved you; go in peace."
—Luke 7:50

He saved us, not because of righteous things we had done, but because of his mercy. He saved us through the washing of rebirth and renewal by the Holy Spirit.

—Titus 3:5

BIBLICAL KNOWLEDGE

*The **user** has little or no knowledge of the Bible.*

*The **servant** is an active student of Scripture.*

*The **leader** knows the Scripture and teaches others.*

Users have little, if any, Bible knowledge. They know the Bible exists but do not yet recognize it as the divine Word of God. They may attempt to intellectually understand what the Bible says, but are not yet prepared to align their actions and behaviors with scriptural direction.

Servants are an active students of Scripture. When life presents challenges, they look to the Word of God for answers and solutions. They have identified the Bible as a primary resource of information on human relationships, appropriate behavior, connecting with God, and serving others. Servants are constantly seeking a deeper understanding of the Scriptures and what God's plan is for their lives through regular study, memorization, and meditation.

Leaders know and understand Scripture and can quote verses from memory. When a challenge or problem arises, leaders immediately know the passage or story in the Bible that offers a solution. Leaders know how to use the Bible as a teaching tool, as a point of reference, and as a divine communication tool that supports their personal relationship with the Father, Son, and Holy Spirit.

In the beginning was the Word, and the Word was with God, and the Word was God.
—John 1:1

I have become its servant by the commission God gave me to present to you the word of God in its fullness.
—Colossians 1:25

Because it is consecrated by the word of God and prayer.
—1 Timothy 4:5

So Paul stayed for a year and a half, teaching them the word of God.
—Acts 18:11

SELFLESSNESS

*The **user** believes the most important person is "me."*

*The **servant** consistently serves others.*

*The **leader** influences others by modeling Christ's sacrificial love.*

Users are entirely self-centered. They may have had a salvation experience, but they are still trying to understand how that experience relates to them, not to others. Users are constantly making their own self the highest priority in their discussions with God, reading of the Word, and inter-action with others.

Servants consistently put others first. Their actions and conversations reflect a genuine desire to respond to the needs of people. However, servants are typically limited in their scope of influence to the people they can reach out and touch directly.

By contrast, **leaders** influence people well beyond their immediate circle. Leaders understand, model, and teach foundational biblical truths that motivate others to action. Leaders influence others to improve their righteousness, purity, holiness, and service to others. Leaders are willing to sacrifice personally in order to achieve what the Lord has called them to do.

And to put on the new self, created to be like God in true righteousness and holiness.
—Ephesians 4:24

Do not lie to each other, since you have taken off your old self with its practices and have put on the new self, which is being renewed in knowledge in the image of its Creator.
—Colossians 3:9-10

LISTENING TO GOD

The **user** *listens to God based upon his or her own experience.*

The **servant** *listens to God with humility and obedience.*

The **leader** *listens to God with an attitude of prepared anticipation.*

Users typically have a hard time hearing God. They want to align what they think they hear from God, through prayer and Scriptures, with their own personal experiences. They approach God with their own agenda and their own ideas about what they should or could be doing for the kingdom.

Servants begin to understand that in order to align with God you need to approach the throne with humility and obedience. Their own agenda is secondary. God's agenda is always primary. Servants begin to understand what it means to put God in charge. Once we take on a servant heart and attitude, God starts opening new doors of opportunity that far exceed our expectations.

Leaders have learned how to listen with humility and obedience to God's instructions. Leaders understand that consistent humility and obedience will bring them into alignment with God's will for their life. Leader are prepared and eagerly anticipate God's next instructions. Leader are seldom surprised by new assignments, difficult tasks, and seemingly impossible challenges. Leaders see God as a partner, resource, and trusted friend.

Go near and listen to all that the LORD our God says. Then tell us whatever the LORD our God tells you. We will listen and obey.

—Deuteronomy 5:27

My sheep listen to my voice; I know them, and they follow me.

—John 10:27

Then I heard the voice of the Lord saying, "Whom
shall I send? And who will go for us?" And I said,
"Here am I. Send me!"

—Isaiah 6:8

WORLDVIEW

The **user** *attempts to align the Bible with his or her*
own worldview.

The **servant** *lives biblical principles daily.*

The **leader** *follows and promotes biblical principles in*
all aspects of life.

Users usually have a difficult time adjusting to God's
sovereignty and omnipotence. Depending on their age and
background, a new believer usually brings "baggage" to
their relationship with Christ in the form of habits, beliefs,
teachings, and expectations.

Servants have begun to adjust their worldview to biblical truths and teaching and now sees the world through
the lens of Christ and His teaching and demonstration of
serving others.

Leaders embrace a worldview from Christ's perspective
and, more importantly, they teach and encourage others to
also adopt a Christlike worldview.

If you belonged to the world, it would love you as
its own. As it is, you do not belong to the world,
but I have chosen you out of the world. That is

why the world hates you.

—John 15:19

For God did not send his Son into the world to condemn the world, but to save the world through him.

—John 3:17

For since the creation of the world God's invisible qualities—his eternal power and divine nature—have been clearly seen, being understood from what has been made, so that men are without excuse.

—Romans 1:20

THE CHURCH

*The **user** looks to the church for help.*

*The **servant** contributes to the body of Christ.*

*The **leader** strengthens the body of Christ through service and personal sacrifice.*

Users show up in the body of Christ or the church looking for help for their problems. They expect to find friends and solutions. They usually make demands and are disappointed when their expectations are not met in a timely manner.

Servants consistently contribute to the local church and the body of Christ with their service and sacrifice. They use their talents, skills, and abilities to meet the needs of others. They build relationships and alliances that benefit their local church and community.

Leaders challenge people to grow and mature spiritually.

Leaders bring groups together to take on problems and challenges. They sacrifice their personal time and resources for the benefit and strengthening of the entire body of Christ. They influence the body of Christ so they can help people they will never know personally.

Leaders bring groups together to take on problems and challenges.

Now I rejoice in what was suffered for you, and I fill up in my flesh what is still lacking in regard to Christ's afflictions, for the sake of his body, which is the church.
—Colossians 1:24

Husbands, love your wives, just as Christ loved the church and gave himself up for her. . . . After all, no one ever hated his own body, but he feeds and cares for it, just as Christ does the church.
—Ephesians 5:25,29

PRAYER

*The **user** prays when faced with a problem or challenge.*

*The **servant** engages in daily prayer time.*

*The **leader** maintains an attitude of prayer throughout the day.*

Users don't fully comprehend the power of prayer. Users approach prayer as their personal wish list to give God. When everything else fails, users then resort to prayer. Sometimes desperate prayer is sincere and appropriate. However, when all prayer is self-centered it is only marginally effective.

Servants recognize the power of prayer and engage in regular daily prayer times. They set aside time to read the Word, study, and pray about the challenges and opportunities of the day. Servants regularly pray for others. They put the power of prayer to work before circumstances become desperate. Servants' lives are improved through disciplined prayer.

Leaders maintain a constant attitude of prayer. They communicate with God throughout the day, as a person would communicate with a best friend. Whether driving in the car, in a business meeting, traveling in an airplane, or hiking in the mountains, leaders are constantly aware of the presence of God in their lives. Leaders invite God to participate in every aspect of their existence. They take no action or make no decision without first submitting the matter to God in prayer.

But when you pray, go into your room, close the door and pray to your Father, who is unseen. Then your Father, who sees what is done in secret, will reward you.
—Matthew 6:6

Be joyful always; pray continually; give thanks in all circumstances, for this is God's will for you in Christ Jesus.
—1 Thessalonians 5:16-18

Devote yourselves to prayer, being watchful and thankful.

—Colossians 4:2

BATTLES AND CONFLICTS

The **user** *avoids spiritual battles and conflicts.*

The **servant** *recognizes spiritual battles and conflicts.*

The **leader** *actively engages in spiritual battles and conflicts.*

Everyday life is full of conflict. In the Christian life spiritual battles are inevitable. **Users** avoid spiritual battles for several reasons. First they do not recognize the spiritual nature of certain types of difficulties. Second they have not yet learned how to fight using the tools and weapons provided by Christ.

Servants recognize spiritual warfare, but are often intimidated by the nature of the battle and by the potential damage they could sustain if they engage in the fight. They would prefer to turn the battle over to the others and watch from the sidelines.

Leaders actively engage in spiritual battles. They understand the power of God is on their side and they cannot lose. They also understand that, by facing and prevailing in these spiritual battles, they will gain strength and experience for future battles yet to come. They are prepared to make the personal sacrifices necessary in order to be part of the victory celebrations that inevitably occur when spiritual battles are won.

In this you greatly rejoice, though now for a little while you may have had to suffer grief in all kinds of trials. These have come so that your faith—of greater worth than gold, which perishes even though refined by fire—may be proved genuine and may result in praise, glory and honor when Jesus Christ is revealed.

—1 Peter 1:6-7

For our struggle is not against flesh and blood, but against the rulers, against the authorities, against the powers of this dark world and against the spiritual forces of evil in the heavenly realms.

—Ephesians 6:12

For though we live in the world, we do not wage war as the world does. The weapons we fight with are not the weapons of the world. On the contrary, they have divine power to demolish strongholds.

—2 Corinthians 10:3-4

TRUST

*The **user** trusts self.*

*The **servant** trusts others.*

*The **leader** trusts God.*

Who and what we trust defines us. **Users** rely and trust self more than God or others. Those who are reluctant, unwilling, or unable to trust God or other people will not mature spiritually.

Servants trust others and are willing to be vulnerable. They open themselves up to the disappointment that can occur when someone they are serving fails to meet their expectations, rejects them, or takes advantage of them.

Leaders trust God and are never disappointed by Him—even if no one else accepts them. There is incredible power in an absolute trust of the Father God, His Son Jesus, and the Holy Spirit. Great spiritual leaders trust God when they can trust no one else.

Some trust in chariots and some in horses, but we trust in the name of the LORD our God.

—Psalm 20:7

Delight yourself in the LORD and he will give you the desires of your heart. Commit your way to the LORD; trust in him and he will do this: He will make your righteousness shine like the dawn, the justice of your cause like the noonday sun.

—Psalm 37:4-6

For like the grass they will soon wither, like green plants they will soon die away. Trust in the LORD and do good; dwell in the land and enjoy safe pasture. Delight yourself in the LORD and he will give you the desires of your heart.

—Psalm 37:2-4

SPIRITUAL GIFTS

*The **user** seeks to understand his or her spiritual gifting.*

*The **servant** recognizes his or her spiritual gifting.*

*The **leader** operates in his or her spiritual gifting.*

Users seek to understand their spiritual gifts. Spiritual gifts are given to us by God to strengthen the body of Christ. Each one of us is wired differently. Our bodies are different. Our minds are different. Our attitudes are different. But before we can put our gifts to work for God we have to understand what they are. If you are interested in determining your spiritual gifts, try the assessment tool at www.followyourcalling.com. This tool covers all aspects of your personality including your motivational gifts, your personality and behavior styles, your career interests, and your cognitive ability.

Servants recognize their spiritual gifts. God's plan for us always involves the application and stewardship of our gifts. Once we recognize our spiritual gifts we can begin to learn how to apply them effectively with power and authority.

Leaders know exactly what their gifting is. The true hallmark of great leaders is that they operate within the skill set that God has given them. They have learned how to maximize their gifts through rigorous training and preparation, and their influence in the kingdom is multiplied exponentially because they operate in concert and coordination with the Holy Spirit.

So it is with you. Since you are eager to have spiritual

gifts, try to excel in gifts that build up the church.

—1 Corinthians 14:12

And in the church God has appointed first of all apostles, second prophets, third teachers, then workers of miracles, also those having gifts of healing, those able to help others, those with gifts of administration, and those speaking in different kinds of tongues.

—1 Corinthians 12:28

So in Christ we who are many form one body, and each member belongs to all the others. We have different gifts, according to the grace given us. If a man's gift is prophesying, let him use it in proportion to his faith. If it is serving, let him serve; if it is teaching, let him teach.

—Romans 12:5-7

TRANSPARENCY IN RELATIONSHIPS

*The **user** prefers isolation; he or she hides.*

*The **servant** selectively establishes relationship; he or she joins.*

*The **leader** engages and commits to relationships; he or she attracts.*

The body of Christ is built and sustained by relationships. Our primary relationship is with God the Father through Jesus Christ and the Holy Spirit. However, those relationships are never fully realized unless we are willing to connect with others.

Users are typically insecure and isolated from others. They are afraid to build close relationships. Their relationships are typically superficial and only deal with surface issues like the weather, children, sports teams, and politics. Getting beyond this insecurity and isolation usually requires time and effort to build the necessary trust. In today's high-pressure society very few people want to take the time to break free from their isolation.

Servants selectively seek to break their isolation by establishing close relationships with certain groups of people. Subject to certain conditions, the servant will build intimate long-lasting relationships with people of like mind and similar circumstances.

> The leader attracts and sustains long-lasting, powerful personal relationships centered on a common interest to do God's will.

Leaders actively engage in establishing relationships with a wide variety of people. They are unafraid of intimacy and recognize that the power of God is appropriated when brothers and sisters in Christ know and trust each other. The leader's motivation for building relationships is to strengthen the body of Christ. The leader attracts and sustains long-lasting, powerful personal relationships centered on a common interest to do God's will.

He pours contempt on nobles and disarms the mighty.
He reveals the deep things of darkness and brings deep
shadows into the light. He makes nations great, and

destroys them; he enlarges nations, and disperses them.
—Job 12:21-23

*He changes times and seasons; he sets up kings
and deposes them. He gives wisdom to the wise and
knowledge to the discerning. He reveals deep and hidden things; he knows what lies in darkness, and light
dwells with him. I thank and praise you, O God of my
fathers: You have given me wisdom and power, you
have made known to me what we asked of you, you
have made known to us the dream of the king.*
—Daniel 2:21-23

*At that time Jesus said, "I praise you, Father, Lord
of heaven and earth, because you have hidden these
things from the wise and learned, and revealed them
to little children."*
—Matthew 11:25

FAILURE

*The **user** blames others for failures.*

*The **servant** acknowledges failures.*

*The **leader** learns from failures.*

Life is full of failures. Failure is inevitable. Yet how
we deal with failure defines who we are. **Users** typically
blame others for their failures. Many of us have had adversity that caused us to develop bad habits, wrong attitudes,

and improper behaviors. As a result we are failing as parents, husbands, employees, and business owners. We can choose to blame those people or circumstances or we can modify our misguided behaviors. Users typically hold on tight to the concept of blaming others for their problems.

Servants acknowledge their own failures and limitations. The beginning of spiritual maturity is to recognize our shortcomings and failures and begin to correct them. We all have flaws, we all have limitations, we all have attitudes and behaviors that are causing us to fail in the roles and responsibilities assigned to us. We search the Word of God and wise counsel to better understand the root of our failures so they can be removed permanently.

Leaders observe failure first in themselves, then in others. The leader recognizes that failure is inevitable and that each failure is an opportunity to learn. The great leadership author and lecturer John Maxwell has written a book called *Failing Forward* which articulates in great detail the benefits of learning from our failures. Great organizations recognize they will fail every day but also have in place systems and processes to learn from their failures.

Test me, O LORD, and try me, examine my heart and my mind.

—Psalm 26:2

The crucible for silver and the furnace for gold, but the LORD tests the heart.

—Proverbs 17:3

Do not conform any longer to the pattern of this world, but be transformed by the renewing of your mind. Then you will be able to test and approve what God's will is—his good, pleasing and perfect will.

—Romans 12:2

OBEDIENCE

*The **user** listens to the Word.*

*The **servant** is a hearer of the Word.*

*The **leader** is a doer of the Word.*

From birth we are all taught to obey. But our natural inclination for disobedience usually constitutes rebellion to someone in authority. God is the ultimate authority and He has clearly defined His expected behaviors in the Bible. As a Christ-follower, we believe that the Bible is the infallible Word of God and offers an immovable plumb line against which all our behaviors are measured.

Users listen to the Word of God but see no immediate consequence for their failure to be obedient to God's Word and direction.

Servants hear the Word and understand what it means and recognizes that there is a consequence should they choose to disobey. The servant begins to modify their behavior in closer alignment with the Word of God.

Leaders recognize that their only alternative is to be fully obedient to the Word of God. Complete obedience to the Word of God is not possible, as we are all imperfect and flawed. However, leaders are committed through study, prayer, accountability, and discipline to making themselves an instrument of obedience to God's calling on their life.

If you fully obey the LORD your God and carefully follow all his commands I give you today, the LORD your God will set you high above all the nations on earth.
—Deuteronomy 28:1

This has been my practice: I obey your precepts. You are my portion, O LORD; I have promised to obey your words. I have sought your face with all my heart; be gracious to me according to your promise.
—Psalm 119:56-58

See, I am setting before you today a blessing and a curse—the blessing if you obey the commands of the LORD your God that I am giving you today; the curse if you disobey the commands of the LORD your God and turn from the way that I command you today by following other gods, which you have not known.
—Deuteronomy 11:26-28

CONTENTMENT OR STRESS

*The **user** operates under stress.*

*The **servant** controls and tolerates stress.*

*The **leader** rejects and removes stress.*

Stress is an inescapable reality of the twenty-first century. The nature of business is stressful. Running a business, managing people, delivering products and services, competing in the marketplace, and overseeing the infinite details required to operate any successful enterprise is stressful.

Users are consumed by stress. They have no outlet to relieve their anxiety. Stress is their status quo. They have not yet recognized that the peace of God that passes all understanding is available to them if they embrace their relationship with Christ.

Servants control and tolerate stress by recognizing its source and limiting its impact through rest, prayer, studying the Word, and recognizing those circumstances outside of their control.

Leaders are content, humble, and calm. It's not possible to operate as a truly mature leader and allow stress and anxiety to dictate their behavior. Leaders work diligently to remove stress from their lives so they can think and act clearly and not allow their decisions to be clouded by anxiety and fear. The Lord's desire for our lives is that we live stress-free and in complete contentment.

And the peace of God, which transcends all understanding, will guard your hearts and your minds in Christ Jesus.

—Philippians 4:7

But if we have food and clothing, we will be content with that.

—1 Timothy 6:8

I am not saying this because I am in need, for I have learned to be content whatever the circumstances.

—Philippians 4:11

Keep your lives free from the love of money and be content with what you have, because God has said, "Never will I leave you; never will I forsake you."

—Hebrews 13:5

FAITH

*The **user** has faith in what he or she sees and hears.*

*The **servant** has faith in biblical truth.*

*The **leader** has faith that God will supply all his or her needs.*

Faith is an action. Faith requires effort, motion, emotion, and activity. We exercise faith every day just driving down the highway. Without faith we can accomplish nothing.

But the key question is, what is the extent of our faith?

Users have faith in what they see and hear, and very little beyond that. They are beginning to develop a faith in God, Jesus Christ, and the Word of God, but are still tightly attached to only believing what they can see and hear in their own experience.

Servants have begun to experience the impact and

results of faith in biblical truth. Through the lives of those they serve they have begun to understand the power of faith in God. The more they understand it, the more they are willing to operate in it.

Leaders have absolute faith in God to supply all their needs. God is their first and primary resource, and faith in Him is their primary tool. There are several immediate benefits to having total faith in God. The first benefit is that He never disappoints our faith if we truly operate in and understand His will. Secondly, if we place our primary faith in God, we are much less likely to be disappointed in people.

Now faith is being sure of what we hope for and certain of what we do not see. This is what the ancients were commended for. By faith we understand that the universe was formed at God's command, so that what is seen was not made out of what was visible.

—Hebrews 11:1-3

Jesus said to the woman, "Your faith has saved you; go in peace."

—Luke 7:50

GOODNESS

*The **user** treats people well when he or she is treated well.*

*The **servant** avoids situations where he or she will be treated poorly.*

*The **leader** always treats others well, regardless of how he or she is treated.*

Goodness is defined as decency, excellence, friendliness, generosity, righteousness, and wholesomeness. Goodness implies treating others well, courtesy, and proper etiquette. Goodness implies service with a willing heart. People who are regularly treated well (with goodness), generally behave well (with goodness).

Users are typically skeptical of others who treat them well for no apparent reason. Users anticipate that a hidden agenda or a perverse motivation is prompting the goodness with which they are being treated. Users only extend goodness when there is some level of certainty that their behavior will be reciprocated.

Servants generally operate with goodness as long as there is no adversity in the process. The servant is looking for safety and also appreciation, even if it is just a sincere thank you.

Leaders are not looking for recognition or appreciation and has determined to offer goodness regardless of the potential risk to their own reputation or safety.

But the fruit of the Spirit is love, joy, peace, patience, kindness, goodness, faithfulness, gentleness and self-control. Against such things there is no law.
    —Galatians 5:22-23

Surely goodness and love will follow me all the

days of my life, and I will dwell in the house of the LORD *forever.*

—Psalm 23:6

Do not let the floodwaters engulf me or the depths swallow me up or the pit close its mouth over me. Answer me, O LORD, *out of the goodness of your love; in your great mercy turn to me. Do not hide your face from your servant; answer me quickly, for I am in trouble.*

—Psalm 69:15-17

KINDNESS

*The **user** can be abrasive.*

*The **servant** carefully regulates compassion toward others.*

*The **leader** has unlimited compassion for others.*

Kindness seems to be a simple action. It is not. Kindness can be defined as gentleness, compassion, patience, and caring. The **user** may be very intense and abrasive, rarely demonstrating kindness and compassion.

The **servant** has learned the value of giving compassion, but is restrained in deciding which people and circumstances to extend themselves.

The **leader** has learned to become attentive to the emotions and feelings of others, extending themselves freely and without reservation, giving wholeheartedly to others.

Consider therefore the kindness and sternness of God: sternness to those who fell, but kindness to you, provided that you continue in his kindness. Otherwise, you also will be cut off.

—Romans 11:22

They prey on the barren and childless woman, and to the widow show no kindness. But God drags away the mighty by his power; though they become established, they have no assurance of life.

—Job 24:21-22

Therefore, as God's chosen people, holy and dearly loved, clothe yourselves with compassion, kindness, humility, gentleness and patience.

—Colossians 3:12

SELF-CONTROL

*The **user** lacks self-control.*

*The **servant** recognizes the need for self-control.*

*The **leader** embraces and practices strict self-control and self-denial.*

Self-control equals discipline. Discipline is the process of focusing on a task or activity until the desired result is achieved regardless of distractions or interference. **Users** may have many gifts and abilities, but they are not willing to submit to the disciplined training required to bring those talents to their highest and best use.

Servants have developed a degree of personal discipline and recognize the benefit in exercising self-control. They generally are mature and committed, serving in their jobs and ministries faithfully.

Leaders are known for their selfless discipline. Regardless of their area of expertise, they have made extraordinary sacrifices to become accomplished and skilled.

Individuals with this type of commitment to discipline will ultimately find the Lord placing them in significant leadership roles.

Like a city whose walls are broken down is a man who lacks self-control.

—Proverbs 25:28

People will be lovers of themselves, lovers of money, boastful, proud, abusive, disobedient to their parents, ungrateful, unholy, without love, unforgiving, slanderous, without self-control, brutal, not lovers of the good, treacherous, rash, conceited, lovers of pleasure rather than lovers of God.

—2 Timothy 3:2-4

Rather, he must be hospitable, one who loves what is good, who is self-controlled, upright, holy and disciplined.

—Titus 1:8

PERSEVERANCE

The **user** *quits faith challenges easily.*

The **servant** *quits faith challenges when they become difficult.*

The **leader** *pursues faith challenges regardless of their personal cost.*

Perseverance is my favorite word in the Bible. Perseverance means keeping on despite all the adversity, setbacks, opposition, challenges, and unexpected problems. It is the essence of both the Christian life and of business. Anytime we step out in faith we are vulnerable to adversity and failure. Problems are part of life. The only question is whether we have what it takes to persevere and overcome them.

> Perseverance means keeping on despite all the adversity, setbacks, opposition, challenges, and unexpected problems.

The **user** has great ideas and wonderful intentions, but rarely has the perseverance necessary to make the great idea a reality.

Servants typically have a point at which they will throw in the towel and allow the opposition to defeat them. There are times and circumstances where pushing through and persevering for a doomed cause may not be prudent or wise. What we need to ask ourselves in these circumstances is: Am I quitting because I am not willing to continue because of selfish motives or am I quitting because, regardless of how long and hard I work, we will not achieve our desired result?

Leaders rarely, if ever, stop pursuing their goals and dreams, regardless of the obstacles, time, sacrifice, and costs. The key difference in leaders is that they usually have a clear, precise image of their destination and keep it firmly planted in front of them at all times. It is much easier to push through and persevere and bring others with you when the objective is clear. Nehemiah had a clear objective of restoring the wall around Jerusalem. Noah had a clear objective of building an ark. Moses had a clear objective of leading his people out of Egypt. Jesus had a clear objective of saving the souls of all humanity. They all persevered to accomplish their objective.

Consider it pure joy, my brothers, whenever you face trials of many kinds, because you know that the testing of your faith develops perseverance. Perseverance must finish its work so that you may be mature and complete, not lacking anything.

—James 1:2-4

Therefore, since we are surrounded by such a great cloud of witnesses, let us throw off everything that hinders and the sin that so easily entangles, and let us run with perseverance the race marked out for us. Let us fix our eyes on Jesus, the author and perfecter of our faith, who for the joy set before him endured the cross, scorning its shame, and sat down at the

*right hand of the throne of God. Consider him who
endured such opposition from sinful men, so that you
will not grow weary and lose heart.*

—Hebrews 12:1-3

Table 6.1: **SPIRITUAL MATURITY LEVELS**

	user	servant	leader
SALVATION	been through	models and promotes	maintains an intimate relationship
BIBLICAL KNOWLEDGE	little or none	active student	knows and teaches others
SELFLESSNESS	"me"	serves others	sacrificial
LISTENING TO GOD	based upon own experience	with humility and obedience	with attitude of anticipation
WORLDVIEW	attempts to align Bible with own worldview	lives biblical principles daily	applies biblical principles in all aspects of life
THE CHURCH	looks to for help	contributes to the Body	strengthens the Body
PRAYER	only when a problem	daily prayer time	prayerful attitude all day
SPIRITUAL BATTLES	avoids	recognizes	engages
TRUST	trusts self	trusts others	trusts God
SPIRITUAL GIFTS	seeks to understand	recognizes	operates in
TRANSPARENCY	hides	joins	attracts
FAILURE	blames	acknowledges	learns from
OBEDIENCE	listens	hears	does
CONTENTMENT	operates under stress	controls and tolerates stress	rejects and removes stress
FAITH	in sight	in biblical truth	in God
GOODNESS	reciprocates	seeks appreciation	regardless
KINDNESS	can be abrasive	careful	compassion
SELF-CONTROL	lacks	recognizes need	practices
PERSEVERANCE	quits easily	quits when difficult	continues regardless

CHAPTER 7

THE ACQUISITION OF COMPETENCE

Wisdom is supreme; therefore get wisdom.
Though it cost all you have, get understanding.

— Proverbs 4:7

In the thirty-sixth chapter of Exodus, we read about the point in history when the Lord instructed Moses to build the tabernacle. He was charged with building the place where the Lord's presence would dwell. But Moses had no idea how to build such a structure. He was called and gifted in many ways, but he was not a skilled craftsman. So God directed Moses to two men who were gifted with the competence and skills required to build the tabernacle.

So Bezalel, Oholiab and every skilled person to whom the LORD has given skill and ability to know how to carry out all the work of constructing the sanctuary are to do the work just as the LORD has commanded.

—Exodus 36:1

Bezalel and Oholiab were skilled, competent craftsmen. Their competence was recognized and valued by God. They were put in charge of building the tabernacle and their job was to instruct, coordinate, and oversee all of the craftsmen in order to build the tabernacle according to the specific instructions that the Lord had delivered to Moses.

It should not surprise us that God values competence. After all, it is He who gives each one of us unique abilities and giftings, with the intention that we develop them for His purpose. "Do you see a man skilled in his work? He will serve before kings; he will not serve before obscure men" (Proverbs 22:29). This passage in Proverbs clearly states that competence is of high value. Someone who is competent, someone who is skilled, will serve before Kings and not before obscure men.

What exactly is competence? In life we all go through a progression of learning and development. First, we begin life in a state of ignorance. Then, through education and opportunities that are offered, we can work to achieve a level of competence and ability. Finally, through commitment, dedication, and discipline, we have the potential to achieve excellence.

At the point of ignorance, we know nothing. When we reach competence, we then have developed a skill or an ability that is marketable and valuable. When we achieve excellence, we now possess a level of competence and skill that allows us to perform in the very top of our fields of endeavor. There is a great deal of emphasis placed on excellence in our society. However, reaching true excellence, though an admirable goal, is not easily achievable for everyone. Excellence, as defined here, usually requires a lifetime of dedication and a disciplined focus, as well as a God-given gift and skill in one's area of ability.

The 10,000 Hour Rule

How is competence gained? Unfortunately, there are no shortcuts to competence. It requires work, discipline, time, learning through failure, and a consistent focus and commitment to the process.

In his book, *Outliers*, Malcolm Gladwell defines something

he calls the 10,000 Hour Rule. Simply stated, the 10,000 Hour Rule establishes that no one is truly competent until they have spent 10,000 man-hours developing that skill or ability. To bring this into focus in terms of a normal individual in the marketplace, ten thousand hours equals forty hours a week, for fifty weeks a year, over the course of five years. Gladwell's premise is this, "To establish a marketable skill or competence requires at least ten thousand hours of dedicated discipline work and concentration." I would wholeheartedly agree.

My wife and I live in Colorado Springs—the home of the U.S. Olympic Committee. Many athletes train for the Olympics here in Colorado Springs. These world-class athletes, who are often legitimate contenders for an Olympic medal, will easily spend ten thousand hours or more in arduous training during the years prior to even qualifying for their Olympic event.

These athletes all strive for excellence. However, they do not have the luxury of defining excellence simply by virtue of their hard work, their dedication, or their attitudes. Their level of excellence is ultimately determined when they compete. There is only one gold medal. And for those who compete on this stage, only the gold medal defines excellence—everything else is just competence.

What I do know to be true is that while excellence is an admirable goal, competence is an absolute requirement to affect Kingdom Impact. Gladwell confirmed what I have often observed and learned over the years.

It takes five years, or ten thousand hours, to train and fully develop a competent property and casualty insurance broker. For the purposes of illustrating the process of development in acquiring competence, the following chronological outline is a summary of how the 10,000 Hour Rule is applicable to the specific role of a Property and Casualty Insurance Broker.

THE 10,000 HOUR RULE

Property and Casualty Insurance Broker

1. 1,000 hours – Learns the language.

2. 1,000 hours – Learns about basic insurance products.

3. 1,000 hours – Learns the basic process of assembling an insurance package for a client or prospect.

4. 1,000 hours – Develops proficiency at communicating about insurance products and services.

At this point, the broker has been working in the industry for two years.

5. 1,000 hours – Begins to understand how products and services apply to a variety of industries and exposures.

6. 1,000 hours – Establishes an understanding about underwriting and how decisions are made about what risks might or might not be acceptable. Also

begins to comprehend the inner workings of the claims process.

7. 1,000 hours – Learns how to leverage the relationships between the carriers and the clients to be sure that all parties' interests are preserved.

8. 1,000 hours – Begins to anticipate problems on behalf of customers, clients, and prospects.

At this point, the broker has been in the industry for four years and is comfortable with the insurance products, the delivery process, and the inevitable politics of selling.

9. 1,000 hours – Begins to understand what is needed to differentiate themselves in the marketplace. Now has enough experience to recognize unique, specific ways to better serve clients and to take advantage of market opportunities.

10. 1,000 hours – Starts to develop process management systems that allow professional service for customers, accurate representation of carriers, and wise allocation of time.

It is important to mention that I have known a number of very sharp individuals who accomplished all of these objectives in less than ten thousand hours. However, they were exceptions to the rule. Everyone is unique, but this outline represents a very accurate average.

It is interesting to note that there is strong biblical support for this concept of the 10,000 Hour Rule. An evaluation of the Gospels, by comparing dates, times, and places where Jesus engaged the disciples, reveals the following conclusions:

◆ The disciples spent a total of three and a half years with Jesus.

◆ Three and a half years equals 1,277 days.

◆ Based upon the assumption that Jesus spent ten hours per day, seven days per week actively training His disciples, that equals a total of 12,777 hours.

◆ Then subtracting the forty days Jesus spent in the wilderness, we find that Jesus spent slightly more than twelve thousand hours training His disciples.

Jesus recognized the need to develop competence in His disciples. They had to go through a learning process in order to possess the skills, knowledge, and understanding necessary to effectively spread the gospel.

Jesus recognized the need to develop competence in His disciples.

David is another biblical example of the 10,000 Hour Rule. He practiced both his music and hunting skills extensively as a shepherd from the age of seven until he was eighteen—nearly four thousand days. We know he killed a bear and a lion. We know he spent an extensive amount of time singing to calm the sheep. There is no way to be certain, but it is highly likely that David had thousands of hours of experience with both his harp and his slingshot. The development of those skills was not an accident. God saw to it that David would acquire those competencies so that they could be used for His honor and glory.

We also see the principles of the 10,000 Hour Rule at work in the life of Joseph. From the time he was put into captivity until the time he entered Pharaoh's service was thirteen years. During those years he learned many practical lessons in human nature from his brothers, Potiphar, Potiphar's wife, the jailer, his cellmates, and ultimately from Pharaoh. He also learned lessons on administration, organization, management, and influence. Again God saw to it that the circumstances in Joseph's life built the competencies Joseph would need. In Joseph's case, if you take into account the unique circumstances of his life, going from ignorance to competence in preparation to do God's appointed works of service required more than thirty thousand hours of training.

In my own case, I have been an insurance professional for more than thirty-eight years and have averaged approximately twenty-two hundred hours of work per year. My total experience as an insurance professional exceeds eighty thousand hours. My wife has been a mother and homemaker for thirty-nine years. As most of us realize, the work of a wife and mother begins the moment her feet hit the ground in the morning until she closes her eyes at night. The typical homemaker, wife, and mother works more than five thousand hours per year. My wife of thirty-seven years has more than 100,000 hours of experience.

Nine Core Competencies

You may be wondering, *why is competence needed?* There are several reasons. First, as believers, we are of little use to the kingdom of God unless we have a competence that He can put into action for His honor and glory. Moses sought out Bezalel and Oholiab because they were competent in their skills and trade. Also, the marketplace in which you offer your services requires that you have an area of competence in order to be employed. The reality is that your level of influence, your compensation, your relationships, and your legacy will all be tied directly to your level of competence.

Unfortunately, too many Christian business owners today are not fully competent in the skills required to operate a successful business. All too often, someone with a technical skill becomes disenchanted with their employer and decides to launch out and start their own business. Being a cook at a restaurant and operating a restaurant are two entirely different skills. Selling insurance and operating an insurance company are two entirely different skills. Being a carpenter and operating a general contracting firm are two entirely different skills.

I sold insurance for five years before I opened my own insurance operation. It took another five years, during which I learned some very difficult lessons, before I became fully competent in operating that insurance company profitably.

There are nine specific skills that are necessary to operate a successful business venture. The primary skill, or core competence, is the core deliverable of the business. In a restaurant the core competence is food preparation and delivery. In an insurance operation the core competence is selling insurance policies. In a contracting firm the core competence is building structures.

It is usually assumed that if someone starts a business they have a high degree of competence in the core deliverable of that business. However, in addition to the core deliverable of every business, there are eight other critical competencies, common to every business. These competencies include planning, marketing, sales, finance, human resources, systems, leadership, and administration. A business without some level of competence in all of these areas has no chance to survive.

Within the Christian business community this creates a significant problem. We've already learned that as a Christian business owner, your business is your ministry. But the reality is, if you are not competent in operating your business, your testimony will be marginalized and you'll ultimately have an adverse impact on the kingdom. For this reason, God requires competence. And competence requires commitment and time.

Choose my instruction instead of silver, knowledge
rather than choice gold, for wisdom is more precious

*than rubies, and nothing you desire can compare
with her.*

*"I, wisdom, dwell together with prudence; I possess
knowledge and discretion. To fear the LORD is to hate
evil; I hate pride and arrogance, evil behavior and perverse speech. Counsel and sound judgment are mine; I
have understanding and power.*

*"By me kings reign and rulers make laws that are
just; by me princes govern, and all nobles who rule on
earth. I love those who love me, and those who seek
me find me.*

*"With me are riches and honor, enduring wealth and
prosperity. My fruit is better than fine gold; what I yield
surpasses choice silver. I walk in the way of righteousness, along the paths of justice, bestowing wealth on
those who love me and making their treasuries full."*

—Proverbs 8:10-21

Grace Is Not Enough

There are two harsh realities that I have come to understand about competence as it relates to business.

1. Competency comes at a price, but will never
   cost you more than incompetence.
2. Grace is not a substitute for competence.

This statement may not be very popular in some churches, but it is true. *Grace is not a substitute for competence.*

For many believers, that goes against everything they think and believe about how God's kingdom works. But while grace is the foundation of all that Christ did for us, it is not enough to affect Kingdom Impact. Grace is not a substitute for hard work. Grace is not a substitute for

Grace is not a substitute for competence.

knowledge and learning. Grace is not a valid marketplace strategy. Grace is not a business tool. Grace is not a business strategy. There is no grace in the marketplace.

The definition of grace is "unmerited favor." We are saved by grace. As Christians we are saved by the unmerited favor of Christ's blood on the cross. We did not and cannot earn our salvation—but although we are unworthy, it is given to us freely. Unfortunately, we live in a fallen world and God's concept and grace is not transferable to our marketplace relationships. There is no grace for gravity. There is no grace in the principles that allow an airplane to fly; the aerodynamics that keep an aircraft airborne are very exacting. The principle of grace in our personal relationships only works when it is freely given, but becomes a cancer if it becomes an expectation.

Unfortunately, many Christian business owners operate on the premise that they will be given "grace" for their lack of skill or competence. Make no mistake, there is no grace in the marketplace. You must be able to deliver your products and services to a standard of competence at least equal to that of your competitors, or you will quickly cease to exist.

The marketplace rewards high levels of competence and punishes incompetence ruthlessly. This is not a law or a regulation that you can amend or appeal—it is a fact of reality as predictable as the sunrise. The marketplace sets its own rules, but fortunately it does value what God values.

In life we grow from ignorance to competence and ultimately to excellence if we dedicate ourselves to disciplined and focused attention to our God-given gifts, talents, and abilities. This process is critical. Think about the last time you traveled on a commercial airline. You probably took it for granted that the pilot was competent. At some point in their life, the pilot did not know how to fly and was completely ignorant. Then, over a period of time, through rigorous training and practice they reached a level of competence that allowed them to take on the responsibility as a pilot in command of a commercial airliner.

Additionally, we know and understand that their competence is continually evaluated and assessed by a regulatory agency that has the authority to revoke their pilot privilege if their competence deteriorates. Of all the pilots in the world, the top 5 percent might be considered "excellent," but we as the passengers have no way to know or understand or evaluate the criteria that might make them "excellent." We assume they are all competent. Would you be interested in boarding a commercial airline whose pilots were given "grace" for their marginal competence?

If we want to compete in the marketplace as a business, organization, or ministry, and thereby expand God's influence in the world through Kingdom Impact, we must be willing to dedicate ourselves to mastering the nine core competencies we mentioned earlier: the core deliverable of the business, planning, marketing, sales, finance, human resources, systems, leadership, and administration. Becoming competent in each of these areas greatly improves the likelihood the organization will survive. Most small businesses have adequate competence in three to four of these areas, and little if any competence in the others. Great, thriving businesses are highly competent in all nine areas and constantly challenge themselves to improve.

If you intend to grow and sustain a profitable business, your business operations competence will be challenged daily. It will be a requirement that you constantly improve your competence if you expect to succeed. However, regardless of the measurement guidelines offered in this text, the marketplace will ultimately evaluate your competence.

The Survivor, The Successful, The Significant

In order to acquire a greater level of competence, we must have a realistic understanding of our current abilities. But how do we measure competence? Much like spiritual maturity, competence is in many ways an intangible aspect in our lives. In order to address this question, we can use specific definitions that measure competence as it relates to business operations. Those definitions are tied to three specific competency levels we call the **survivor**, the **successful**, and the **significant**.

The **survivor** is the emerging business that has not yet reached marketplace credibility or profitability on a consistent basis. The **successful** business has been around long enough

that its survival is no longer in doubt and it is generating adequate profits and cash flow. The successful business is meeting the needs and expectations of its owners, employees, vendors, and customers. The successful business has a presence in its community but has a limited ability to impact local or global culture.

The **significant** business generates excess cash flows and profits. It is a leader in its industry and a key employer in the communities that it serves. The significant business impacts not only its own community but also the communities of its vendors, suppliers, and customers. It sets the competitive bar for its industry peers. The significant business has the resources and influence to create sustainable Kingdom Impact.

When creating a set of metrics to establish levels of business competency, it is necessary to create definitions that are easily understood and represent readily recognizable signposts in the process of growing the business competency of the organization and its leadership. Measuring business competency can be done in the context of many different factors that influence the growth and success of the business. We will focus on the behaviors of the owner and leaders of the business. Our definitions describe their levels of business competency and skill.

We will also identify characteristics of the cultures of those businesses as it relates to their methods of operation, their systems, their influence, their profits, and their cash flow. As we develop these ideas in more detail you will see a pattern emerge. For the sake of simplicity we have provided these comparisons on a single chart as part of the support material of this book (see page 178). However, in order to fully comprehend and appreciate The Compound Effect it will be necessary to review these comparisons in detail. That is what we will do in the next chapter.

CHAPTER 8

THE SURVIVOR, THE SUCCESSFUL, THE SIGNIFICANT

Make level paths for your feet and take only ways that are firm. Do not swerve to the right or the left; keep your foot from evil.

— Proverbs 4:26

Before we begin evaluating the different levels of business competency, I want to clarify that the information that follows is the culmination of thirty-seven years of observing more than fifteen thousand businesses and being personally involved in thirteen different enterprises at some level of ownership or management. The characterizations that follow come from observations of all types of businesses—those that succeeded beyond the wildest imaginations of their ownership, as well as businesses that failed miserably, despite the best intentions and prayers of everyone concerned. These stories that follow will help clarify what business competence looks like and how it is developed over time. But for every illustration, there are at least ten to fifteen more that confirm the principles of this measurement tool. (For a summary of these priciples see Table 8.1 on page 178.)

TIME

*The **survivor** wastes time.*

*The **successful** uses time.*

*The **significant** creates time*

We all have the same amount of time. Everybody has twenty-four hours a day, seven days a week, fifty-two weeks in a year. The difference between failure, success, and significance is how we use our time. An emerging business owner starting a new venture seems to have no time at all because there are so many things to accomplish and never enough time for most of it.

The **survivor**. A friend and client, Kenneth, is a gifted and talented carpenter. He consistently wastes time. He wants to be a home builder, but is terribly disorganized. He makes promises he couldn't possibly keep unless he worked twenty-four hours a day. Instead of delegating responsibility for the details of building a home, he attempts to solve all of the small problems himself. He wastes enormous amounts of time driving and talking to clients and can barely make it through each day. Unfortunately, he will likely fail in his home-building business.

The **successful**. Another construction client, Steve, is extremely organized. He uses time well. He spends most of his time training and delegating responsibility to his employees and subcontractors. He has a strict accountability process for construction schedules and budgets that he enforces personally and rigorously. He uses his time judiciously. His company consistently completes their projects on time and on budget. Many of his customers regularly refer business to him. He has the luxury of being able to select his customers and says no to the ones he does not want to deal with. This is certainly a successful company, but because it is organized around the talent and skills of the owner, this business cannot currently grow beyond the owner's ability to directly manage and control day-to-day operations.

The **significant**. Tom is the CEO and minority stockholder of a significant manufacturing company with gross revenues of more than $100 million annually that employs in excess of nine hundred people and distributes their products in five continents. Many of the people who work in the manufacturing plants are second-generation employees. These plants are scattered in rural Midwestern communities where they are the largest employer in the county. This manufacturing company was an insurance client for a number of years. I learned a great deal from Tom. Perhaps most significantly, Tom doesn't just use time, he *creates* time.

Tom works at his position of CEO four days a week, twelve hours a day, eight months of the year. He is an incredibly competent CEO with both an academic pedigree and extensive operational experience. His greatest strengths are his people skills. He serves on the board of three charitable organizations and the board of regents of his state university. He is active in politics and the Alumni Association of the prestigious university where he received his MBA. Tom has an abundance of time, influence, and resources.

With all of this, he and his wife of thirty-five years still manage to spend at least two months of the year traveling to visit their children and grandchildren who live in various parts of the world.

*The **survivor** wasted time and his business died a painful death.*

*The **successful** used time and succeeded nicely but worked very hard.*

*The **significant** created time and directly influenced more than fifty thousand people.*

CASH FLOW

*The **survivor** has marginal cash flow.*

*The **successful** has consistent cash flow.*

*The **significant** has excess cash flow.*

The **survivor**. As a brand-new commercial insurance brokerage firm, the greatest threat to our existence was marginal cash flow. When we billed a new customer, they typically paid us immediately. However, existing customers who added vehicles or new exposures to their policies typically did not pay us until they received a bill. In order to keep some accounts we would be forced to extend credit for thirty days or longer. We became a bank. Some of our customers promised to pay us and never did. For every dollar that went uncollected we had to sell one hundred dollars of new premium to make up for the one dollar of bad debt. Cash flow was an everyday battle. Finding the money to pay our bills, including payroll every fifteen days, was a constant struggle. I learned the hard way that we could not afford to be a bank.

The **successful**. Once we decided to stop being a bank, our cash flow improved. No matter how valuable a customer was, we learned that we could not afford to keep them if they would not pay their bill in a timely manner. We offered premium finance plans for those who needed to pay their premiums over time and we learned how to fire those customers who wouldn't pay their bill. Very quickly our cash flow became positive. We were spending less time dealing with accounts receivable and more time generating new business and taking care of our good customers who did pay their bills. Eventually we arrived at a point where we had enough excess cash flow that we were able to make investments in new opportunities, including acquiring additional insurance offices and hiring new employees to grow our business.

The **significant**. Later in my insurance career I became the president of an insurance company owned by a bank. The bank provided the funds to acquire an existing insurance agency along with the funds needed for us to overcome twelve months of negative cash flow as we began to grow the company. After twelve months we began generating positive cash flow and over the next five years grew the company from nine employees in three locations to thirty-five employees in five locations. Businesses with excess cash flow have the luxury of choosing from among multiple opportunities to grow and prosper. They also have the luxury of having a positive impact on their employees, their communities, their nations, and the world.

CUSTOMERS

The **survivor** *is begging for customers.*

The **successful** *is selecting customers.*

The **significant** *is creating customers.*

Customers are the lifeblood of every business.

Customers are fickle.

Customers are always right even when they are not.

Customers make the rules.

Customers like to be appreciated.

Customers appreciate value.

In the process of training and managing insurance sales professionals, we defined their place in the organization within the context of the type of customers that they served. They were known as the "Rookie," the "Pro," and the "Superstar."

The **survivor**. The Rookie, or brand-new insurance sales professional, was expected to write insurance on anything that walked and talked and paid a premium. As a Rookie they had not yet earned the right to be selective about their customers.

The **successful**. The Pro, who had usually been in the business a minimum of five years and often ten or more, had earned the right to select their customers. As a Pro they typically had long-term client relationships and went to great lengths to be sure that those relationships were served efficiently and professionally.

The **significant**. The Superstar usually operated in a specific vertical market and had a unique product or service that attracted and created new customers. The Superstar identified a need for a differentiated insurance product or service that solved a unique problem within the insurance marketplace. Once the unique insurance product or service is offered, it automatically attracts new customers.

COMPETITION

*The **survivor** fights the competition.*

*The **successful** is the competition.*

*The **significant** embraces the competition.*

Competition is everywhere. It is an integral part of business and life. Strong ethical competition in any industry serves to raise the bar of quality and service for the customer. Competition also gives businesses the opportunity to differentiate themselves from their peers. How a business responds to competition clearly defines their status.

Competition is everywhere. It is an integral part of business and life.

The **survivor**. I have been a skier for more than fifty years. I have watched the evolution of ski equipment from wood skis, leather boots, and leather strap bindings, to today's modern composite-shaped skis with high-tech bindings and boots.

Twenty-five years ago I saw a snowboard for the first time. They were crude, flat boards with jury-rigged bindings adapted to traditional ski boots. I was not impressed. It looked dangerous—and it was. Many ski resorts would not allow snowboards on their slopes. A few daring souls decided to start manufacturing fiberglass snowboards in direct competition with the ski companies. Most of those snowboard companies failed.

They fought the competition—the ski industry—and lost.

The **successful**. A few snowboard companies managed to persevere and began to grow and thrive. They successfully competed with the ski industry by marketing their product to a younger generation who was looking to be differentiated from their parents. In time these companies became a legitimate competitive force. Today the snowboard industry represents almost 40 percent of the lift tickets sold in ski areas across the United States. Just recently, one of the last ski resorts that had always prohibited snowboards on their mountain relented and lifted their restriction. Their lift ticket purchases immediately jumped by 20 percent. Snowboard manufacturers became serious competition for the ski industry manufacturers.

The **significant**. Today the snowboard industry is a sophisticated and powerful worldwide market force. They have redefined what happens on and around the mountains of the world. They have redefined winter sports. They are now a significant—and extremely popular—part of every Winter Olympics. Twenty years ago there was no such thing as a half pipe or terrain park within a destination ski resort. Snowboarders have defined their own culture through their language, dress, and code of conduct. Snowboards and snowboarders have become significant and are here to stay. They are the primary driver for the recent resurgent growth of the ski resort industry. The ski industry, and more specifically the ski resort industry, now embraces snowboarding as a vital part of their continued success.

At the ripe age of fifty-four I attempted to take up snowboarding, since several members of my family favored snowboards. I failed miserably and painfully. I will be satisfied to remain a skier for life. Some things are not supposed to change.

KNOWLEDGE

The **survivor** *believes he or she has knowledge.*

The **successful** *seeks knowledge.*

The **significant** *shares knowledge.*

Knowledge comes in many forms. The best knowledge is usually acquired through personal experience. However it can also be gained through reading, study, and observation. To build and sustain a viable enterprise, a business owner must have an adequate amount of knowledge in multiple business disciplines. It is assumed that if we are starting a new business, we have the technical knowledge necessary to deliver the products and services for the business we intend to start.

A residential home builder is expected to know something about carpentry and construction. The restaurant owner is assumed to know something about food preparation and service. Each business has its own set of core technical competencies. We need to be absolutely certain that we have the necessary core competence knowledge before we launch our own business.

The **survivor**. As a rookie insurance agent I was desperate and hungry to write new business. I would submit insurance applications for any risk that would talk to me. One day I was at a local restaurant and asked if I could quote their insurance. They said, "Absolutely, we pay a lot for insurance. When can you give us a quote?"

In my ignorance I thought it would be simple. I thought I had the knowledge and experience necessary to sell insurance to this risk. After all, how difficult could this be? I completed an application and sent it into the company. The following Monday morning, my office door opened and in walked my company representative with the application for the restaurant in his hand. His comment to me was, "I'm sorry this is not an acceptable risk."

However, he didn't stop there; he invited me to go with him so he could show me why this was not an acceptable risk. We drove to the restaurant, borrowed a ladder from one of the contractors drinking coffee inside, and crawled up onto the roof of the building. When we got to the top of the building I was appalled. The grease, dirt, and grime caked on the vent over the stove was at least four inches thick. We then went down into the kitchen and looked at the breaker box and electric wiring. The building had been built in the 1920s and none of the electrical services had been updated.

Needless to say, after I had been given this new knowledge I understood why this was an unacceptable risk. I began the day believing I had knowledge and by the end of the day understood that I did not have enough knowledge. A standard characteristic of businesses in survival mode is that they think they know what they need to know in order to be successful. They usually don't. This is a dangerous place to be.

The **successful**. After several years in the insurance industry I began to build a surplus of experience and knowledge. I knew the process of writing insurance on restaurants. I had learned not to waste my time or the time of my underwriters submitting unacceptable risks. I had developed enough knowledge and experience to pinpoint what type of risks would be acceptable. I began to understand policy language, policy service, and claims administration. The more I learned, the more I realized I did not know. I had a successful and growing insurance agency. I was blessed to have a number of key mentors in my life who were willing to answer my constant questions. Every day I focused on learning as much as I could from the people and situations I encountered.

The **significant**. Bob was the owner of a small independent claims adjusting firm located several doors down from my office. Two or three times a week Bob and I had coffee and we would discuss insurance claims. Bob was an artist of human understanding. Over his career Bob had adjusted and settled tens of thousands of insurance claims. His very successful business was built on the delicate process of spending the insurance company's money prudently, while providing satisfaction to the policyholder or claimant. Through Bob's knowledge and experience I learned that insurance policies are subject to interpretation and that settling insurance claims was far more art than science. What

I learned from Bob could never be gleaned from a book or manual. By answering my questions and expanding my knowledge, Bob made me a more successful and better insurance professional. Bob shared his knowledge with me voluntarily, patiently, and passionately.

Today, I have thirty-seven years of commercial insurance experience. I, too, am passionate about sharing my insurance knowledge. Not long ago I reached a point in my career where I had the responsibility for the sales and marketing of $1 billion commercial insurance premiums. I've become a source of functional knowledge and experience in the industry. As I watch young insurance professionals struggle with the challenges of making a living, I find great satisfaction in being able to share my knowledge and experience and encourage them to continue to improve their skills and abilities.

PLANNING

The **survivor** *does minimal planning.*

The **successful** *does consistent planning.*

The **significant** *does long-term, detailed planning.*

Planning is essential to completing any complex task from building a house to winning a gold medal. It is no different when starting a business. A plan becomes a template or guideline by which you evaluate opportunities and make decisions. A plan gives you a target. If you aim for nothing you will hit it. A plan will help you build a business that serves you, versus you getting stuck serving your business. A plan will help you prioritize and focus your daily personal and business activities.

A plan gives you a target.

The **survivor**. Kris is an electrical contractor. Seven years ago, he was forced to start his own company when his employer, a large electrical contractor, laid him off. He never had any type of plan except to feed his family. His business had serious challenges. He worked more than eighty hours per week and was barely squeaking by. He was frantic, stressed, and desperate.

The **successful**. Kris attended a Weavers class for thirteen weeks and then went back to work. When I saw him again two years later, I barely recognized him. He was smiling, fit, trim, and happy. He said, "I did what you said and made a plan but it didn't quite work so I changed it. That worked better but I had to change it again. It still wasn't what I wanted so I changed once more, and then things finally clicked." The whole process took about eighteen months and the result was that his business was flourishing. "My customers love me, I am making twice as much money, I work about forty-five hours per week, I get to spend weekends and evenings with my family, and I just bought a sailboat!" As a survivor Kris did almost no planning. Today Kris's business is quite successful.

The **significant**. Significant businesses plan consistently. They hire or employ experts to forecast trends in the changing economy, changes in consumer preferences, or the impact of new technologies so they can position themselves to expand their businesses. Great companies use detailed and consistent planning to focus on strategic and tactical positioning so they can establish or expand their marketplace presence and increase revenues, profits, and shareholder value.

No business will succeed without some level of planning. Not planning is not an option. Sloppy planning results in sloppy work and little, if any, long-term value. Great planning and careful attention to detail results in outcomes that are noticed, appreciated, and highly valued.

In his heart a man plans his course but the Lord determines his steps.

—Proverbs 16:9

Commit to the Lord whatever you do, and your plans will succeed.

—Proverbs 16:3

RESOURCES

The **survivor** *wastes resources.*

The **successful** *applies resources.*

The **significant** *creates resources.*

Resources come in many forms—including time, money, relationships, raw goods, talents, skills, knowledge, experience, ethics, morals, and convictions. As a business owner, your primary objective is to deploy the resources at your disposal as efficiently as possible to create profits and additional resources. He who makes the best use of the resources at his disposal makes more resources.

The **survivor**. A start-up business usually does not even recognize what resources it has at its disposal let alone how they should be deployed. One of the most compelling reasons for writing a business plan is to organize the resources at our disposal and be sure that they are not wasted. An emerging business usually has limited resources, the most limited being time and money. Businesses in "survivor mode" consistently waste their resources because they lack the planning, knowledge, and experience necessary to know how to put those resources to the best possible use.

My first business was an independent insurance agency. We did an extensive business plan using large columnar accounting worksheets to calculate our projected income and expenses. I needed to save money and made the decision to create my own accounting system. This was well before the era of personal computers, let alone programs like QuickBooks.

For the first five months we used our checkbook as our accounting system. I had taken an accounting course in college but barely passed and did not fully comprehend how to create a double entry bookkeeping system. Our college course taught us theory and concept, not experience and application. I believed the system was adequate until the business began to grow and we started paying taxes. We were also encountering issues with billing, collection, and vendor payables.

I was finally forced to seek out an accountant. When the smoke cleared, four things had happened:

1. I had installed a simple, off-the-shelf industry financial management system that provided complete monthly financial reporting, including aged accounts receivable, balance sheets, and profit and loss statements.
2. My payroll taxes were corrected and current.
3. My bill from the accountant was thirteen hundred dollars to go back and correct all of the errors I had made in the first five months of operation.
4. The entire process took a couple of hours of my time every day for ten weeks to correct. Once the new system was in place, the monthly fees were less than one hundred and fifty dollars, including what I paid the accountant at the end of the year to file our tax returns.

I had wasted resources by not having a complete accounting system from day one of our new business. From that point on I never started a new venture without installing a complete accounting system before the first dollar of income was generated.

The **successful**. Successful businesses are careful and

deliberate with how they apply their resources, especially time, money, and relationships. As a business grows, resources are gradually accumulated. One of the most vital, though expensive, resources to acquire is human capital. Trained, motivated, trustworthy, and competent employees are required for any business to achieve even modest success. Successful businesses breed successful people. Successful people build relationships. Successful businesses take the time to train and motivate their employees. In our modern economy, employees and the relationships they create will either make or break a company. The following is an example of what can happen if business fails to manage their human resources (people) well. This company misapplied their resource of relationships.

ABC Bank Holding Company had a prevailing old-school philosophy: no outside ownership, no shared profits, and all compensation was tied to seniority or cost of living—not productivity or production. The company was owned and controlled by a family who lived on the earnings of the holding company.

Over a period of several years, a number of key executives and senior loan officers left the company for more lucrative opportunities. One started his own chartered bank operation, taking a substantial percentage of ABC Bank's customers in a specific market. Others went to work for competing financial institutions. In each case, customers loyal to those individuals moved their business. As a result, the holdings and earnings of ABC Bank have diminished in value by more than 50 percent.

Conversely, a major competitor in the same market, who has a philosophy of shared ownership, shared profits, and compensation tied to productivity and unit profitability, has doubled in size over the past six years. This successful company, that has wisely applied its resources, has continued to grow in this adverse economy.

The **significant**. Significant businesses create new resources. When a business reaches a certain critical mass and a consistent level of profitability, it has the luxury of creating new resources. This might include accumulating operating capital to acquire a competitor, or opening a new product line, or investing in additional training for key employees.

When we sold our first insurance operation to a bank holding company, I was invited to join a much larger, reputable regional insurance firm. Their commitment to coaching, training, and compensating was considerable. I was part of a group of four new sales people hired within a two-month period. The firm spent ninety days training all of us in its specific marketing, sales, and customer service culture, all the while paying very reasonable base salaries and benefits to all of us.

We embraced their system and their culture wholeheartedly. Twenty-five years later, I have yet to come across a more effective insurance sales training and management system. Within twenty-four months, I had created in excess of $400,000 in new revenues for the company using their methods and systems. Their compensation plan rewarded us handsomely for every dollar of new revenue we created. As a group, the four of us created $1.4 million in new annual revenues over that time span and served to increase the profits and market value of the company by 25 percent.

Significant businesses invest wisely in new resources that generate not only revenues and profits, but also incredible value to all their shareholders. Life is good when you work for a significant company that models biblical business leadership and shares appropriately with the people who make the business a success.

OWNERSHIP

The **survivor** *– the owner is the key employee.*

The **successful** *– has key employees other than the owner.*

The **significant** *– business operates without the owner present.*

One of the greatest hurdles to growing a business from survivor to successful to significant, is the willingness and ability of the owner to adapt to new roles as the business grows. As a company grows, the owner must recognize the need to change his or her role and embrace the opportunity to acquire broader business competencies and skills. If the owner is unwilling to grow and change, the business will become stagnant and probably fail.

The **survivor**. Chuck is a home renovator. He is a

competent and qualified craftsman and excellent "people person." His business was thriving, but there were not enough hours in the day for him to fulfill all of his commitments. Chuck needed to take on employees to keep up. He started hiring his friends and people he knew in the industry. The business grew but Chuck was working even harder. His quality of life suffered and he was not making any more money, in fact he was losing money. It wasn't long before he was discouraged and broke.

The **successful**. Chuck had a choice—he could take the time to develop the business management skills he needed to operate a successful business with ten or more employees, or he could terminate his employees and go back to doing what he already knew how to do as a craftsman.

Chuck spent thirty hours in training class learning very basic business management skills. He received instruction in the areas of planning, human resources, finances, leadership, marketing, sales, business systems, and administration. Chuck's wife attended several sessions as well. After prayerful consideration and some additional one-on-one counseling, Chuck and his wife developed a very specific business growth plan and made the decision to terminate all but two of their employees. They are now four years into their plan. Their two employees have taken on considerable additional responsibilities, allowing Chuck the opportunity to develop his business management skills and devote his time to marketing, sales, planning, and systems.

Since implementing their plan, the revenues of the company have increased, the business is profitable, and they have entered several new markets. Chuck's new operational systems have made the business much easier to manage and the quality of his family life has dramatically improved. Chuck's business has grown from survivor to successful. The entire process has taken six years.

The **significant**. Scott is a chronic entrepreneur. He sees opportunities where other people see obstacles. He believes his ministry is to create business opportunities for others by finding solutions to difficult problems. Scott has established several significant businesses that enable him to offer strong financial support to multiple Christian organizations.

When Scott discovers a new opportunity, he looks for the right people, then builds a business around those individuals and makes himself available when needed. Many of his businesses are in Pacific Rim countries and are operated by natives. Scott has put systems and processes into place that allow him to monitor the daily activities of these companies from anywhere in the world using state-of-the-art technology. He visits each business several times per year and communicates with his managers on a continuous basis. He has built trust and rapport with his managers and willingly shares profits and earnings when the businesses prosper. Scott will freely admit that the businesses probably operate better without him there than if he were trying to run them himself.

PROFIT

*The **survivor** operates at a loss.*

*The **successful** produces a profit.*

*The **significant** generates excess profit.*

Profitability in business or ministry is not optional. Every enterprise must take in more revenue than it spends. This includes churches, ministries, nonprofits, governments, and families. Any doctrine or political statement to the contrary is a false teaching. Profitability is biblical.

Who serves as a soldier at his own expense? Who plants a vineyard and does not eat of its grapes? Who tends a flock and does not drink milk?
        —1 Corinthians 9:7

When the plowman plows and the thresher threshes, they ought to do so in the hope of sharing in the harvest.
        —1 Corinthians 9:10

Remember this: Whoever sows sparingly will also reap sparingly, and whoever sows generously will also reap generously.
        —2 Corinthians 9:6

There seems to be a mistaken notion that a "nonprofit" organization has some operational advantage, which allows it to purchase their goods and services below market cost.

The only advantage a nonprofit might have is a preferential tax treatment on its earnings. Viable nonprofit organizations have all the same operating costs as traditional businesses including rent, payroll, payroll taxes, utilities, marketing, postage, and technology. For a nonprofit to remain viable, it must operate profitably.

The **survivor**. Businesses in survivor mode usually operate at a loss for a period of time. But if they fail to reach profitability, they will go out of business. Based on statistics, 67 percent of all start-up businesses do not sustain profitability and ultimately fail. Achieving and sustaining profitability should be the highest priorities of every start-up enterprise.

The **successful**. Successful businesses are built upon sustained reinvested profits. As their company grows, wise business owners dedicate a portion of their annual profits to the continued growth of their business. Prudently reinvested profits yield additional profits in the future and also serve to stabilize and protect a business from the adverse economic cycles that will inevitably come.

The **significant**. Significant businesses generate excess profit. Excess profit means excess taxes. Wise stewards of these excess profits usually choose to protect these excess profits from taxes by applying them to various national and international philanthropic organizations. This is where the wealth of nations can be used for sustained global Kingdom Impact.

Within the Weavers teachings on biblical business leadership, profitability is one of nine leadership commitments. The Weavers commitment to profitability is:

I will plan, establish, and maintain a profitable venture that meets all its obligations and honors God with its stewardship. I will fairly and appropriately reward those who contribute to the growth and profitability of our business. I will establish and provide a financial legacy that serves future generations of my family and the kingdom of God. I will tithe from my earnings and give my time and financial resources as led by the Holy Spirit.

CHANGE

*The **survivor** reacts to change.*

*The **successful** anticipates change.*

*The **significant** creates change.*

The one thing that is certain in life is that things change. In business, change happens every day. How we react to change says much about our leadership and the maturity of our organization.

The **survivor**. Flying an airplane effectively is about controlling the motion of the plane in three dimensions. When I was a novice student pilot, I was definitely in "survival mode." I was always reacting to the constant changing motion of the airplane, and I definitely was not in control. In pilot lingo I was "behind the airplane." But once I had accumulated twenty-five to thirty hours of training with my instructor, I began to be able to anticipate the changes that were taking place around me and react in such a way that I could keep the airplane under control, most of the time.

Eventually, my instructor was satisfied that I could handle critical changes in such a way as to not jeopardize my life or the airplane. After flying for about fifty hours, I earned my private pilot's license. Over the past thirty years I've accumulated more than fourteen thousand hours of pilot-in-command flight time. I am now proficient enough in several airplanes to completely understand how to control them with a fair amount of competence. I have learned how to stay "ahead of" the airplane. The survivor business reacts to change.

The **successful**. Business today happens at light speed. The landscape of products, services, competition, regulation, finances, people, and politics literally changes by the minute, by the hour, and by the day in any given workweek. The successful business has been around long enough to have persevered through these kinds of changes a dozen times or more. They start to anticipate and pre-pare for what's going to happen next. Successful busi-nesses are rarely surprised by the changes that take place in their business environment. The successful business anticipates change.

The **significant**. Significant businesses do not let changes take place arbitrarily, or without intention and planning. A significant business has built-in processes and systems to manage arbitrary changes in such a way that they do not affect the stature, the culture, or the profitability of the business. When noticeable change takes place in a significant business it is an intentional change designed to achieve the desired result: increased profits, larger market share, better productivity, or improved customer service.

Not long ago I had the privilege of listening to the president of a well-known, prominent, privately held company as he discussed their company culture and their competition. The focus of his presentation was how his company had changed over the past sixty years and how it expected to continue to change over the next sixty years. He did not see his competition as his primary business adversary. His strongest adversary was the internal tendency within his own company to become complacent with the processes, systems, and methods that had made them into a significant company with $3 billion in annual revenues. He made this comment about how he viewed the subject of change within his company: "When the rate of external change exceeds the rate of internal change, chaos is imminent." The significant business is effective at maintaining the proper balance by intentionally creating change.

TACTICS

The **survivor** *plays defense.*

The **successful** *plays offense.*

The **significant** *coaches the team.*

In many ways, businesses are like teams. Even a small, one-man operation cannot survive without engaging other people in various roles that directly affect the productivity and profitability of the business. The cultural differences between the survivor, the successful, and the significant business are comparable to the behavior that occurs on a baseball, football, or soccer field. This analogy relates not only to the organization, but more specifically to the leadership.

The **survivor.** My family has been actively involved in youth sports for more than thirty years. There were many times when my wife and I sat on the sidelines and watched helplessly as our children's teams were clobbered by teams made up of kids who were quite a bit older than our own. If you've not been through this experience, it is humbling, to say the least. Our children were outmatched, with little hope they could defeat their opponent. They were in survival mode—with their main objective to play good defense and try not to let the other team score too many goals.

Some people might say that our children should not be put in a situation where they can get clobbered. But sports are a great training ground for the realities of life. And reality is that life isn't always "fair." The good news is that in a matter of one year, our kids were the ones doing the clobbering. They learned how to hang on, survive to play another day, and developed greater skills by being forced to compete against the "big guys." Businesses in the survivor mode get clobbered every day. Like our children, they have not yet reached a maturity level where they could legitimately compete against the "big guys." They have no choice but to play defense.

The **successful**. Once our children got organized, grew up a little bit, and started learning the skills and strategies of the game, they stopped getting clobbered and started scoring points and goals—much to the joy and delight of their parents and coaches. Success breeds success and confidence. Successful teams and successful businesses are always on the offensive. The only way to win is to score more points than your opponent. To finish first, you have to have more wins than any other team. Continuing to play great defense can make a significant contribution to winning, but becoming a successful business or team requires that we stay on the offensive all the time.

The **significant**. Youth sports are fun, entertaining, and full of valuable life lessons. Many children who compete aspire to become professionals, but only a very small percentage actually fulfill that dream. To reach the significance of becoming a professional, the athlete needs to understand and respond to direction and coaching. Truly significant athletes all have great coaches who help them mature in both the physical and emotional aspects of their sport.

Championship teams are created by coaches who understand how to get the most out of their individual players. The same applies to significant (champion) businesses. Significant businesses are run by great coaches who assess the talents and skills of their teams, understand how to designate positions or roles, prepare them through rigorous training, motivate them to work as a unit, and accept the responsibility for both failures and successes. Great leaders of significant businesses are usually great coaches.

MISTAKES

The **survivor** *constantly makes mistakes.*

The **successful** *learns from mistakes.*

The **significant** *anticipates mistakes.*

Mistakes are inevitable. The first challenge with any mistake is to admit that you made it. In recent years we have witnessed moral and ethical lapses at the highest level of both business and ministry leadership. These mistakes caused incredible loss and heartache to the employees, stockholders, and customers of those companies. In the case of ministries, the damage to the credibility and influence of the body of Christ is immeasurable. Moral and ethical accountability should be a requirement at all levels within every organization.

The **survivor**. Surviving businesses consistently make

mistakes. When I started my first insurance company, I did business with people who never paid me, I failed to keep accurate transactional records, I sold policies that did not have the correct policy terms, I failed to ask all the right questions when trying to sell a new account, and made many incorrect assumptions about the insurance claims process. However, I was very willing to accept responsibility for all those mistakes and fix them. Fortunately, we did succeed and become profitable in spite of my mistakes—but those profits would have happened sooner and been larger had I not made them.

The **successful**. The leaders of successful businesses learn from their mistakes. I had been operating or managing various businesses for more than thirty years when I was approached by a bank holding company and asked to start an insurance operation. The bank owners had some very specific ideas about how an insurance operation should function within a bank holding company. But their thinking was flawed. I knew they were about to make a serious mistake, not because they weren't good bankers and business people, but because they did not fully comprehend the operating business model of an insurance company. Fortunately, I had made plenty of mistakes within that industry and had learned from all of them. We built a thriving operation primarily because I had learned what not to do.

The **significant**. Significant businesses expect and anticipate mistakes, and install systems and processes to deal with them appropriately. Large companies build specific boundaries around human error. Given the volume of transactions in the course of everyday business, errors happen. Significant businesses work diligently to keep those errors to a minimum and make sure the cost is negligible.

CONFLICT

The **survivor** *creates conflict.*

The **successful** *avoids conflict.*

The **significant** *resolves conflict.*

Conflicts arise every day in the business environment. The nature of business is risk, and with risk usually comes conflict. But how those conflicts are resolved will ultimately determine the long-term fate of the business. Constant strife and conflict within a company or organization is a cancer that undermines the productivity and profitability of the enterprise. The tension that's created when trust is broken, when deadlines are not met, and products and services do not meet expectations drains the energy and diverts the focus of the employees. Managing conflict is a critical skill for any company that hopes to get past the survival stage.

The **survivor.** An emerging business tends to create more conflict because of its lack of organization, planning, and experience. When employees are allowed the opportunity to make critical decisions without proper training, accountability, and oversight, the result is an environment ripe for conflict. Businesses that operate in fear of conflict because one or more employees or owners have volatile emotions are usually doomed to failure. A survivor business without a structured mechanism to manage conflict will fail.

The **successful**. On the other hand, successful businesses manage conflict. They see conflict as an opportunity for the business to grow and improve. Strong business leaders learn how to manage the emotion out of conflict. They encourage the interactions and dialogue that results from these issues, recognizing that differences of opinion within an organization are healthy, while unresolved personal conflict is a serious hindrance to the organization.

The **significant**. Significant businesses are consummate mediators and arbitrators. They usually have an individual within the organization whose sole job is to resolve conflict. For emotional conflicts involving personalities, human resource professionals are tasked with offering a resolution process. For operational conflicts, ownership and senior managers are expected to investigate and resolve the issues. When conflicts arise from external sources, such as competitors, regulators, and suppliers, the resolution process may involve multiple levels of management from corporate officers to line supervisors.

Conflict will exist within any enterprise. How are you dealing with the conflict in your organization? Are you the main cause or part of the solution? Do you allow those conflicts to become a cancer or a catalyst? If they are a cancer, they could be terminal. If they are a catalyst, they will define your legacy.

CULTURE

The **survivor** has an uncertain culture.

The **successful** has a defined culture.

The **significant** has a secure culture.

The **survivor**. Why is organizational culture important? The culture of a business is its personality. Organizational culture can be established either by accident or by design. But the culture of a business or ministry ultimately becomes its reputation and is a direct reflection of its leadership. Organizational culture evolves over time. The culture of an organization is the sum of the direction and behaviors of leadership and employees or members, the internal systems and procedures of the organization, the physical environment and the interactions and interrelationships of the people, and the success of the enterprise over time. A business in the survivor mode typically has not yet established a culture.

The **successful**. How can we recognize and understand the culture of an organization or business? By meeting the people who work there as well as those who interact with the organization as customers, vendors, and suppliers. What do those people say about the organization? Does the external message of the company or ministry match their conversation? Are they loyal or critical? Are they optimistic or pessimistic? What do they believe about the organization?

Every business or organization—including families, businesses, churches, schools, sports teams, military units, and governmental units—has a culture either by accident or by design. A successful business usually has a well-defined culture that has been ingrained into the operations and employees of the company.

The **significant**. The image and brand of an organization defines its external reputation. The culture is the internal reputation and the operational reality of the enterprise. The significant business or ministry has a confident and secure culture that carries extraordinary influence with all the stakeholders. The culture pervades its thinking, planning, hiring, and problem solving. Companies with a secure culture recognize its weaknesses and limitations and are rarely surprised when adversity knocks on the door. Its employees are always ready to unite behind ideas rather than money, as the protection of the principles of the organization's culture becomes a more important motivation than personal gain.

COMMUNITY

The **survivor** *depends on the community.*

The **successful** *supports the community.*

The **significant** *transforms the community.*

The **survivor**. The first thing most new businesses do is join their local Chamber of Commerce. They seek help within their local community to find reputable professionals including lawyers, accountants, insurance agents, and other professional advisors to help them structure their enterprise. After the business is organized, they use the Chamber community to begin looking for customers, seeking referrals, doing advertising, and as a point of reference to support the viability and credibility of their business. Most businesses cannot get past the survivor mode without strong support from their local community.

The **successful**. As a business grows and matures into a successful venture, the owner may become a more active member of his or her local Chamber of Commerce by participating on committees, helping with events, and encouraging others to become members. Owners of successful businesses support community charitable events and become active members in civic organizations. Successful business owners also have the capacity to support their local church through tithes and offerings, sponsor missions outreach, and offer their resources in times of crisis and turmoil.

The **significant**. Significant businesses that employ large numbers of people or have access to great resources can literally transform their communities. A small rural community in eastern Kansas became the site for a Walmart distribution center in the mid-1990s. This Walmart distribution center, which covers more than 400,000 square feet and services Walmart stores within a five hundred-mile radius, now employs more than five hundred people from the surrounding communities. The leadership of this facility are all actively involved in community and civic activities and regularly offer the resources of the company to the many underprivileged families and children in the area.

EXIT STRATEGY

The **survivor** *has no exit strategy other than failure.*

The **successful** *is considering possible exit strategies.*

The **significant** *has a defined perpetuation plan in place.*

The **survivor.** The reality is that very few start-up companies have a defined exit strategy other than failure.

The **successful.** Often, even very successful companies don't have a solid exit strategy. Eric, a good friend of mine, operates an automobile repair shop that is quite successful and has been around for more than twenty years. The business occupies a very high profile piece of real estate on a major thoroughfare in the city.

However, Eric's health has deteriorated significantly in the past two years. His family is dependent on income generated by the business. Yet, none of his children have an interest in taking over the business. None of his employees have the financial wherewithal to buy the business or the real estate. Eric has approached several of his nearby competitors and asked if they would be interested in buying his business. They have been either unable or unwilling to consider his offer.

One of the key factors working against him is that Eric

has never trained anyone else to manage the business. He is the primary manager and his presence is required a minimum of eight hours per day, six days per week. At this point, Eric's feeling is that God will take care of everything, so there is no pressing need to find a buyer or a manager to replace him. Unfortunately, this is a flawed strategy, since Eric's health condition is potentially fatal. Should the unthinkable happen without a defined exit strategy in place, his family would be forced to sell the assets of the business including the real estate, without the benefit of his knowledge and wisdom and well below its value.

The **significant**. Everyone who owns a business will eventually leave that business—the only question is when and how. Not having a defined exit strategy is poor stewardship of that resource. Very early in my professional career I established a relationship with the owner of a financial institution who had a family of five children. When I met him, the children ranged in age from fourteen to five. That was thirty-five years ago. Thirty-five years ago this individual established a trust to transfer his assets to his children when he turned seventy years of age. Thirty-five years later those assets are valued in excess of $100 million and they have been successfully transferred to his children by a specific process set up thirty-five years earlier. Those five children have the opportunity to take the assets that their father has provided and potentially multiply them by a factor of 300 to 400 percent.

Every business should have a defined exit strategy, carefully thought out, planned, and executed.

LIVES

The **survivor** *drains lives.*

The **successful** *sustains lives.*

The **significant** *transforms lives.*

The **survivor**. Larry launched a car wash and auto detailing business. He picked a marginal location and lacked the capital necessary to hire the required help to service his customers in a timely manner. His target market was the recreational vehicle community. He established relationships with a number of recreational vehicle dealers. They provided a steady stream of motor homes and campers to be cleaned and detailed before they went to the dealers' lots.

Larry found himself with more work than he could handle, so he began hiring casual laborers. Because this unskilled labor force required constant supervision, Larry found himself working seventy to eighty hours a week. His wife and four children saw very little of him. And when he finally did make it home he was so exhausted and irritable his family was not happy to see him. The business was draining his life. Despite receiving strong encouragement to close or sell the business because of the collateral damage that was being done to his family by the demands of his business, Larry ignored that advice and ended up divorced.

The **successful**. Bob grew up working in his father's ski rental shop, which he now owns and operates. This shop is a landmark on Main Street in a Colorado mountain town. Generations of families have rented skis from Bob and his father since the 1970s. Generations of high school students have worked in Bob's ski shop. Bob's family has been actively involved in the community and contributed generously and consistently to the community outreach programs and civic projects. Through their business, Bob and his family have sustained lives in their community.

The **significant**. Compassion International is in the business of transforming lives. Compassion International is a ministry run according to solid biblical business principles. Its foundational mission is transforming the lives of children in poverty for Christ. Today they are actively involved in the lives of 1.2 million children across the globe. This would not be possible without an effective and efficient business structure. Despite the downturn in the economy in 2008 and 2009, this ministry is thriving and is executing a comprehensive business strategy that will enable them to serve five million children by the year 2015. Significant businesses transform lives.

OPPORTUNITY

The **survivor** *craves opportunity.*

The **successful** *discovers opportunity.*

The **significant** *attracts opportunity.*

The **survivor**. When I started my first insurance agency, I was craving any opportunity I could find to write a new insurance policy. I knew that if I did not find an opportunity, my children would not eat. I knocked on doors; I pleaded; I pursued any new lead that I could think of. I also spent time networking with friends, organizations, and existing clients trying to determine where new opportunities might exist.

The **successful.** Later on in my insurance career, I began discovering new insurance opportunities. One time while prospecting, I met with a company that was in the process of acquiring a recreational vehicle manufacturing facility. They had run into problems trying to purchase product liability insurance. In the process of designing an insurance program for this company I discovered that the entire recreational vehicle industry was in the same situation. The process of finding affordable, appropriate product liability insurance was quite tedious, the market very limited, and the problem was virtually universal for every RV manufacturer. I discovered a great opportunity to serve the recreational vehicle industry by providing a more competitive, more comprehensive product liability insurance policy. We joined the recreational vehicle industry association and in less than three years developed eighteen new clients representing almost $400 million in annual recreational vehicle sales. I discovered an opportunity and took advantage of it.

The **significant.** When my insurance career finally brought me into a management role with a national brokerage firm, my responsibilities included helping the organization create specific programs of insurance designed for selected industry segments. Our firm was responsible for more than $1 billion of insurance premiums in the western half of the United States. Within our region we had more than sixty industry-specific programs.

One of the more successful programs was designed for public and private schools. Our firm provided the property, professional liability, workers compensation, and automobile insurance to 50 percent of the school districts in one particular state. Our producers and their staffs were on a first-name basis with most of the school superintendents and their chief financial officers. We actively supported and participated in their annual conferences, legislative initiatives, employee training programs, and their safety and risk management policies. Our firm carried a strong reputation within the school district community and over time we increased our market share in the state by more than 200 percent. By virtue of our size, our competence, and our reputation we attracted opportunity.

SYSTEMS

*The **survivor** has no systems.*

*The **successful** is constructing systems.*

*The **significant** has proven systems.*

Great businesses are built upon great systems. Businesses that are dependent on people instead of systems are vulnerable to failure when those key people are no longer available to make the company operate.

The **survivor**. A business in a start-up or survivor mode typically does not have any proven operating systems in place. One of the compelling reasons for someone, who wants to start a new business, to purchase a franchise is to take advantage of the proven systems offered by the franchisor. For example, purchasing a carpet-cleaning franchise provides a start-up business owner with systems and processes that have been proven to work for other franchise owners. Many people look at the cost of purchasing a franchise and see the price as excessive. However, the cost to learn that business and establish those systems on their own might be four to five times more than purchasing the franchise. If you are considering the purchase of a franchise ,it is advisable to look at those who have a large number of successful franchisees who have all achieved their success by adhering to the systems offered by the franchisor.

The **successful**. Successful businesses have built their own operating systems. These systems are in place for virtually every aspect of business including planning, sales, marketing, human resources, finance, administration, and leadership. Within a successful business there is a constant effort to improve systems and make them more efficient and effective. Successful businesses study their competitors carefully to determine what systems they might be able to adapt to their own company. Successful businesses are constantly examining how their employees utilize and interact with their operating systems. A critical facet of any system is the training provided to the employees to maximize the effectiveness of that system.

The **significant**. Significant businesses are built on tried and proven systems. However, danger exists when operating systems become too rigid and fail to adapt to changing technologies and marketplace conditions. Great companies constantly challenge themselves and work diligently to improve their operating systems. Significant companies carefully measure the effectiveness and the productivity of their people and their operating systems, looking for any advantage that can be gained by making their systems more efficient and responsive.

LEGACY

The **survivor** *has a marginal legacy.*

The **successful** *has an emerging legacy.*

The **significant** *has a defined legacy.*

Legacy is what you leave behind when you're gone. Your legacy is how you are remembered. Your legacy is the condition of the people within your sphere of influence when you are no longer part of their lives.

The **survivor**. Almost without exception, businesses that never get out of the survivor mode leave a negative or, at best, marginal legacy. Businesses that just barely survive and never become successful or significant take an incredibly negative toll on the lives of the people around them. The collateral damage that occurs to families when the mother and father are totally consumed by keeping the business operating can be devastating. Children are neglected, principles and ethics are violated, family priorities are preempted, and finances drive virtually every life decision that is made. Every business will go through the survivor mode, but they must move on if they expect to leave a positive legacy.

The **successful**. A successful business has a legacy that is emerging. Typically, a successful business has a culture, a way of doing business by which it is recognized. That recognition is tied to its attitude toward its employees, customers, and reputation within the community it serves. As a business grows, its culture begins to define its legacy. Successful businesses, with a positive culture that improves and enhances the lives of the people within their sphere of influence, will begin to leave a positive legacy. Successful businesses with a negative culture that uses people, takes advantage of customers, fails to pay its bills in a timely manner, and is constantly under scrutiny by authorities will leave a negative legacy. A good example of this is the situation with Lehman Brothers, which collapsed in 2008 during the financial meltdown. The management of Lehman Brothers left an incredible negative legacy for its employees, customers, the taxpayers of the United States, and its community of investment firms.

The **significant**. Significant companies such as IBM, Microsoft, Ford, and Marriott Hotels all have transformational legacies. These companies have not only impacted their employees and customers, but they have transformed the communities that they serve, the quality of life in other nations, and the standards of performance and excellence within their industries. None of this transformational legacy can take place without business competence, excellence, and corporate profits. These companies recognize their moral obligation to leave a positive legacy and have created systems to ensure that their legacies remain positive.

Table 8.1: **BUSINESS COMPETENCE LEVELS**

	survivor	successful	significant
TIME	wastes	uses	creates
CASH FLOW	marginal	consistent	excess
CUSTOMERS	begging	selecting	creating
COMPETITION	fights	is	embraces
KNOWLEDGE	believes	seeks	shares
PLANNING	minimal	consistent	long-term detailed
RESOURCES	wastes	applies	creates
OWNERSHIP	key employee is owner	key employees other than owner	operates without owner present
PROFIT	operates at a loss	produces profit	excess profit
CHANGE	reacts	anticipates	creates
TACTICS	defense	offense	coaches
MISTAKES	makes constantly	learns from	anticipates
CONFLICT	creates	avoids	resolves
CULTURE	uncertain	defined	secure
COMMUNITY	depends	supports	transforms
EXIT STRATEGY	none	considering	defined
LIVES	drains	sustains	transforms
OPPORTUNITY	craves	discovers	attracts
SYSTEMS	none	constructing	proven
LEGACY	marginal	emerging	defined

CHAPTER 9

THE PURPOSE OF MEASUREMENT

Therefore let us go on and get past the elementary stage in the teachings and doctrine of Christ (the Messiah), advancing steadily toward the completeness and perfection that belong to spiritual maturity. Let us not again be laying the foundation of repentance and abandonment of dead works (dead formalism) and of the faith [by which you turned] to God, with teachings about purifying, the laying on of hands, the resurrection from the dead, and eternal judgment and punishment. [These are all matters of which you should have been fully aware long, long ago.] If indeed God permits, we will [now] proceed [to advanced teaching].

— Hebrews 6:1-3

The Lord has blessed me with many mentors and teachers over the course of my life and each one of those represented a divine appointment. I met Keith while I was seeking a solution to a business problem for an insurance client. At the time, Keith was in his early seventies and had recently retired from a major international corporation as its director of product safety.

Keith was an incredibly generous and gentle family man, a patient teacher, a godly man, and a great friend. He was loyal to his company for more than forty years and possessed infinite wisdom about corporate politics, business realities, thorny legal issues, life lessons, and the finer points of golf. He was passionate about people.

Keith had a father's heart. He and I connected at a very special level the first time we met. He went out of his way to be sure that I understood the length and depth and breadth of the concepts he taught me. I was the sponge; he was the garden hose. Although Keith was well paid by my client, the value of what I learned was priceless. What he taught me has never lost its relevance.

Keith's company is well known throughout the world, manufacturing equipment for the agriculture, construction, and consumer markets. Keith was responsible for the product safety of every product line. In an era when product liability litigation was rampant, Keith had the incredible responsibility of protecting the assets of this publicly traded, multibillion-dollar company from the ravages of plaintiffs' attorneys. My client was seeking advice about how to design and manufacture products in a way that would minimize their exposure to excessive product liability litigation. They were extremely pleased to have a consultant with Keith's credentials and experience.

The Quantification of Subjective Information

Right now, you might be wondering, *What does this have to do with measuring spiritual maturity and business competency?* Keith taught me an extremely valuable skill and process, a disciplined detailed approach he had applied to managing product liability risk. The technical name for this process is called "the quantification of subjective information and decision making." More simply, it is described as assigning a value to a subjective decision or idea, such as a feeling or behavior, in order to better ascertain its relevance and importance. For example, perhaps you have been asked by your doctor about the pain you are experiencing from a particular injury or sickness. He asks you, "On a scale of 1 to 10, 1 being almost no pain and 10 being excruciating, how bad do you really hurt?" By using that criterion to answer the doctor's question, you're using the quantification of subjective information to communicate the level of your pain.

In the case of the products manufactured by Keith's company, the question was, "How do we design, market, deliver, and service a product that is inherently danger-ous in such a way that the operator and bystanders will not be harmed, even when they operate the equipment improperly?" The answer to that question had to take into consideration a variety of variables including the intended purpose of the equipment, the unexpected or unintended human behavior (stupidity) of the operator, the machine's operating environment, the life expectancy of the equipment (sometimes more than fifty years), the marketing and promotion of the equipment, and its service requirements. However, the most important aspect of Keith's responsibility was that all safety and human interface considerations for each product had to be defensible in a court of law should someone sustain an injury inflicted by one of their products.

In the process of designing heavy equipment, agricultural machinery, and consumer products, certain safety features had to be incorporated into those products in order to prevent injury to the operators and bystanders. In the course of making those decisions, there were many conflicting priorities including available technologies, operator training, cost, and functional impairment. Over a period of twenty-five years as a product safety director for this major corporation, Keith had developed a very simple but effective safety evaluation mechanism using "the quantification of subjective information and decision making."

This process addressed all those interrelated issues associated with applying safety features to a piece of agriculture or construction equipment. When properly executed, Keith's processes resulted in the application of innovative and effective safety features on all the company's equipment. More importantly, this safety evaluation and design process was defensible in a court of law. Plaintiffs' attorneys had a difficult time extracting large settlements and punitive damages from his company because of this product safety design program. Keith literally saved his company hundreds of millions of dollars over the course of his career. He was incredibly well-respected and highly revered, not only within his company, but also within his industry and even by his adversaries.

Over a period of several years, Keith taught me the intricacies of this system and the incredible value of "the quantification of subjective information and decision making." At the time I had no idea that this was part of God's plan for my life and my ministry. The Lord had a larger plan for the application of this information than I could possibly imagine.

Measuring Intangibles

When the Lord called me to begin teaching biblical business principles to small groups and emerging business owners, He revealed to me this concept called "The Compound Effect" that He wanted to communicate in His kingdom. This concept applies "the quantification of subjected information and decision making" to the issues of business competency and spiritual maturity. It is a method to measure the Kingdom Impact of a Christian business or ministry. The Compound Effect is the transformational power of business competency and spiritual maturity.

The Compound Effect builds on the idea that both spiritual maturity and business competency can be measured. Churches and religious organizations rarely, if ever, establish metrics or measurements to evaluate the effectiveness of their work. They usually measure things like the number of salvations, or amount of tithes, or number of people attending on Sunday. However, they have historically failed to develop or apply meaningful metrics as it relates to measuring the spiritual development of the individuals in their congregations.

Quantification of Subjective Information

Businesses on the other hand, especially successful businesses, measure everything. In today's highly competitive environment, most successful companies are constantly measuring not only their profits and their sales, but also the intangibles of their customer's behaviors, feelings, and reactions. How many times have you been asked to complete a survey that asks about your satisfaction and whether or not a particular product or service has satisfied your expectations? This information is all very subjective, but absolutely critical to the success of these companies. I have yet to be asked by a church to complete a survey that addressed the status of my spiritual maturity or my satisfaction with their ministry.

In order to measure something that is subjective, we

must first establish definitions and descriptions that can be recognized and contrasted to show their relative difference. For example, in the area of spiritual maturity, The Compound Effect identifies the characteristics of three distinct types of spiritual maturity to be considered in sequence of continual improvement.

We have already discussed the three primary behavioral categories at length. First is "**the user**," a new born-again believer whose mode of behavior is predominantly self-centered. Second is "**the servant**," who has developed beyond the self-centered attitude and is characterized by consistently serving others. And finally "**the leader**," who has developed beyond the servant's role, into a leader of leaders. Assuming that we follow the plan that the Lord has set out for our lives, as we mature spiritually, we will naturally progress from user to servant to leader.

In the process of building anything—whether it's a house or business or relationship—there are always measurements involved. In order to define progress and success or failure, a scale of critical milestones is usually established. When we take a trip, we are interested to know how far we are from the destination. We generally follow a map that plots our course and allows us to determine our progress.

Many of Jesus' parables used critical measurements. His miracles were clearly measurable. However, the numbers were never the reason for the story, they were there only to support the idea or the lesson. Consider the miracle of the fish and the loaves that fed five thousand. The point of the story was not the numbers, but the numbers told the story. With the parable of the talents, the point of the story was not who received what number of talents, but the outcomes that were created by obedience to a principle versus disobedience toward authority and responsibility.

In the process of building anything— whether it's a house or business or relationship— there are always measurements involved.

Facing the Truth

As a young man I was immature. This was evident in my spiritual life, my emotional life, and my relational life. I was certainly not interested in measuring my maturity— or rather, the lack of it. I would have had serious issues with anyone who suggested it. For those same reasons, it is not surprising that there is a natural reluctance on the part of the church to engage in a process of measuring the spiritual maturity of their members.

The unfortunate truth is that immaturity is plainly evident even when it's not acknowledged. Ignoring the reality only creates an even greater vulnerability or weakness in the body of Christ. Part of becoming a mature believer is recognizing the need to evaluate our own maturity and learn how to improve it. The Word of God clearly requires us to mature in our faith. "Perseverance must finish its work so that you may be mature and complete, not lacking anything" (James 1:4).

Keith has gone to be with the Lord. It has been almost twenty years since he taught me these very valuable lessons and skills. These lessons and skills are now being applied in a way that is expanding the kingdom of God. As I reflect on the chain of events that has led me to where I am today, I truly marvel at how God orchestrates relationships, information, and circumstances to achieve His desired results in our lives. We all need to ask ourselves, "What am I learning today that will be used in new and different ways twenty years from now?"

CHAPTER 10

THE COMPOUND EFFECT AT WORK

For though we live in the world,
we do not wage war as the world does.
The weapons we fight with are not the
weapons of the world. On the contrary, they
have divine power to demolish strongholds.

— 2 Corinthians 10:3-4

While researching and developing the concepts for this book, it wasn't long before I began to uncover numerous businesses and organizations that exemplified The Compound Effect. I have included a handful of these in this chapter for the sake of illustrating what these principles really look like in action. Some of these individuals, businesses, and organizations are widely known, others are not. But they are all achieving incredible Kingdom Impact by devoting themselves to improving both their business competency and their spiritual maturity every day.

THE SALVATION ARMY

The Salvation Army embodies the mission of Kingdom Impact—the transformation of people's lives through the application of Christ's love and biblical principles. The Salvation Army operates in 122 countries and provides services in 175 different languages. Its annual budget exceeds $2.6 billion. It has more than one hundred thousand full-time employees and one million volunteers worldwide.

The Salvation Army was founded upon eleven biblical doctrines including the sovereignty of the Trinity—God the Father, Jesus the Son, and the Holy Spirit—and the belief that the Scriptures of the Old and New Testament were given by the inspiration of God, constituting the divine rule of Christian faith and practice.

The sustainability and effectiveness of this ministry is only possible because of its operational competence. It has proven systems in every core area of business competence including planning, sales, marketing, leadership, finance, systems, human resources, and administration. Its systematic development of leadership at the local, regional, national, and international levels has served as the foundation for its 146-year legacy. Its stringent financial accountability systems have enabled the Salvation Army to consistently distribute most of its contributions to the poor and needy around the world. Its finances are audited by outside auditors annually and financial reports are available on request.

Its world-class marketing and sales efforts enable the Salvation Army to raise the necessary funds to accomplish its mission. Its state-of-the-art administrative and logistical support systems enable the organization to offer effective real-time support and resources to natural disasters worldwide. The Salvation Army is always among the first to arrive after natural or man-made disasters such as the tsunami in Indonesia, Hurricane Katrina, the 9/11 tragedy, and the devastating 2011 earthquake and tsunami in Japan. Very few ministries have the organizational infrastructure found within the Salvation Army. This ministry is an organizationally sound business.

The Salvation Army is respected worldwide and recognized across geopolitical and cultural boundaries as a reliable resource in times of desperation and tragedy.

The Salvation Army is founded on biblical principles, but its effectiveness as a ministry is just as dependent on its organizational competence as it is on the power of prayer. On The Compound Effect–Kingdom Impact Scale, the Salvation Army scores as close to 100 as any business or ministry we examined.

THE DOCTOR DON STORY

Don is a prince in God's kingdom in the marketplace. His core deliverable and competency is dentistry. His entire being reflects Jesus. Don is a son, brother, father, husband, grandfather, boss, community leader, and mentor and testimony to many. Don exemplifies the Father's heart.

Don prays daily with his employees and patients. His dental practice provides the financial resources to run a ranch in the Colorado mountains that has become a ministry and a haven for families. He is a prayer warrior who not only petitions God on his knees on behalf of multiple ministries, but also generously offers his financial support as led by the Spirit. Don's business is the platform from which he conducts the ministry of the gospel. He does business for God all day, every day. His spiritual gift is his incredible discernment and tender spirit. He weeps and intercedes regularly for those within his influence. He is one of the few people who calls me regularly just to ask how I am doing in my walk with the Lord. He asks about my business, my family, and my prayer life.

Surprisingly enough, Don's life has not been without challenges or heartaches. Don is a modern-day Job. His faith has been constantly tested by life's circumstances. Not only has he remained faithful to God, but he has maintained his ministry and his testimony throughout all of those trials. His heart for God has never wavered. For those of us who know him well, his walk is a testimony with very few equals.

Don recognizes his marketplace leadership is an integral part of his testimony and the effectiveness of his ministry. He has been a mentor and a model for many men—young and old. He reflects Christ everywhere he goes—his home, his dental practice, his friendships, his relationships, and his ranch. A day stretching fence with Don on the ranch in the mountains of Colorado and talking about things of God is like bathing in the presence of the Holy Spirit. Don is a vessel that overflows with the power of God in the marketplace. Don epitomizes the principles of The Compound Effect.

THE CHICK-FIL-A STORY

In 1946 S. Truett Cathy began selling chicken sandwiches in a small restaurant called the Dwarf Grill in Hapeville, Georgia. Over the past sixty-five years, S. Truett Cathy and his family have built what I refer to as The Church of the Chicken Sandwich. Chick-fil-A has effectively demonstrated the power to transform the lives of people. In 2010 Chick-fil-A generated gross revenues of $3.5 billion, serving chicken to two million people per day in fifteen hundred locations while increasing in store sales by 5.6 percent. Chick-fil-A employed seventy thousand people and donated millions of dollars to various charities and philanthropic organizations.

Chick-fil-A is a business built and operated on biblical principles. Its corporate purpose says, "We strive to glorify God by being a faithful steward of all that is entrusted to us and to have a positive influence on all who come in contact with Chick-fil-A." Customers are served with honesty, integrity, and creativity every day. A life-size bronze statue of Jesus washing the disciples' feet is the centerpiece of the atrium in Chick-fil-A's corporate offices. A smaller version of that sculpture is prominent on the desk of the senior executive of the company. This statue is not just a corporate symbol but truly represents the culture of Chick-fil-A, for S. Truett Cathy is a man of God who values people.

This organization not only serves its customers and employees, but also takes responsibility for the needs of others in the community—locally, nationally, and globally. Through the WinShape Foundation, created by S. Truett Cathy in 1984, the resources of Chick-fil-A are used to serve the needs of college students, at-risk children, underprivileged youth, families, couples, and the unreached people groups of the world. This company and the family that established it are an incredible model of The Compound Effect.

I spent some time recently on-site with a Chick-fil-A store owner in Colorado. This amazing, gracious mother of three has been part of the Chick-fil-A family for twenty-two years. She has a heart to serve. Her income as an owner and partner in this successful Chick-fil-A franchise is substantial. Yet what motivates her is not the economic reward, prestige, or recognition, but her passion to minister to her employees. She shared a statistic that is a profound commentary on our current social condition. In her Chick-fil-A store, 50 percent of the teenage employees are from single-parent homes. Through this business she has the opportunity to minister to the spiritual, emotional, and financial needs of the young people who work in her store.

The Chick-fil-A employee orientation and training program emphasizes discipline, manners, etiquette, customer service, teamwork, and language. Chick-fil-A, like all great companies, has its own language made up of key words that define its product and culture. This is the first time that many of these young people have been encouraged to learn discipline, manners, and etiquette. The Chick-fil-A culture consists of stringent and very specific service-oriented behaviors.

This manager shared with me, "These young people thrive in an environment of discipline, direction, purpose, and caring. They are at a very impressionable age. What we teach them stays with them for the rest of their life. The most rewarding part of my job is to have a young person come back two or three years after they have left the restaurant and tell us what a profound impact we've had on their lives. Our goal is to see transformation in the lives of our employees every day."

Chick-fil-A behaves as though its business is its ministry. By transforming lives through a for-profit business operated according to biblical principles, Chick-fil-A is creating Kingdom Impact. This is an incredible demonstration of what happens when business competency is multiplied by spiritual maturity. This is a vital demonstration of The Compound Effect.

JERRY'S STORY

Jerry is a diminutive man who speaks with halting, thoughtful words. I became acquainted with Jerry through a morning men's Bible study where we shared round tables with eight to ten other men every week. It did not take long for me to build a deep appreciation and respect for the power and conviction of this gray-haired grandfather. This humble, obedient man had a close personal relationship with Christ that he demonstrated and projected through his compassion for people and incredible spiritual insight into the issues that presented themselves at our table discussions week after week.

Jerry is a retired insurance executive. He spent most of his career with a national company as an agent and a district manager. Jerry was a careful and diligent steward of the resources God provided. He did not live extravagantly. Jerry's home and his family reflected the Scripture, "But as for me and my household, we will serve the LORD" (Joshua 24:15). Jerry and his wife raised their children in the fear and admonition of the Lord. He invested in rental properties as part of his retirement plan. Long ago, Jerry and his wife established a "Samaritan fund" which they contributed to every month. This fund was over and above their tithe, and they used it to support ministries and the needs of people as the Holy Spirit led them. Funds were never dispersed without prayerful consideration and always with unity and agreement between Jerry and his wife.

In the mid-1990s, as Jerry began to contemplate retirement, the Lord provided him an opportunity to take a missions trip to Pakistan. During that trip God moved upon Jerry's heart and gave him a burden and passion for the indigenous Christian church in Pakistan. For many years, there has been a small Christian community in Pakistan. They make up less than 4 percent of the population, but this community of Christians is bound by poverty. The political and social reality of Pakistan is that economic enterprise and the higher paying income positions are all reserved for Muslims. Even well-educated Christians have little or no opportunity to advance economically or socially.

Jerry's burden and passion quickly turned into action. Over the past thirteen years Jerry's ministry has established more than three hundred new businesses in Pakistan begun by Christians through micro-enterprise loans. A typical loan is six hundred dollars. Those loans are repaid monthly over two and a half years at an interest rate of slightly more than 15 percent. Each loan is used to create a new for-profit enterprise operated by a Christian who is expected to tithe from earnings and support a local church.

The types of businesses that have been started include a sewing shop, welding shop, bicycle repair shop, herd of milk cows, computer learning center, and numerous retail shops. Each loan immediately impacts an average of seventeen people. It provides for their immediate needs, improves their quality of life, provides resources to assist the church, and elevates their social influence in the local community. Of the more than three hundred loans made during the past thirteen years, there have been only three defaults. The interest income from the loans support the in-country administrative team made up of Pakistani Christian Nationals.

Jerry's vision is to raise $1 million of microenterprise loan funds for Pakistani Christians in the next five years. Over a ten-year period of time that $1 million would serve more than one hundred thousand Pakistani Christians and generate in excess of $150,000 of annual interest income. Keep in mind that the $1 million principal is intended to operate perpetually and be continually reapplied to establish new ventures to Pakistan well after Jerry has gone to be with the Lord.

Jerry's vision and passion, combined with his spiritual maturity and business competency, has enabled the Lord to use him for significant kingdom purposes in Pakistan. Jerry recognizes that he will be unable to continue to travel to Pakistan much longer due to his age. But the Lord has brought several key businesspeople alongside him to see that the vision and mission are accomplished. Jerry's legacy and that of his ministry will be hundreds of thousands of Christians in Pakistan impacting their country for the kingdom of God for generations to come. Now this is Kingdom Impact!

THE COMPASSION INTERNATIONAL STORY

Compassion International is a vibrant, growing ministry transforming the lives of children all over the world through the application of The Compound Effect. Compassion International effectively demonstrates the transformational power of multiplying business competency with spiritual maturity.

The spiritual maturity of Compassion International is well known and documented. Its website, logo, mission, and values clearly reflect Christ and its name personifies its mission to improve the lives of children all over the world. Its corporate culture is built upon biblical principles and is reflected in the work ethic and the attitudes of its employees. Its leadership promotes, demonstrates, and teaches fundamental biblical principles as part of its leadership responsibilities within the ministry.

What is less known and not as easily apparent, is that this is a very professional and productive business enterprise. Creating an infrastructure that effectively and efficiently ministers to the needs of more than 1.2 million children across the globe requires considerable business acumen. The core competency of Compassion is serving children in need. To accomplish this objective there is a specific set of skills required, including a unique language, unique products and services, and a unique distribution system. How well Compassion executes these functions differentiates them from their peer organizations around the world.

However, beyond the core competencies that make this organization unique, there are eight traditional activities that are common to every business. The fact that Compassion International happens to be a ministry does not in any way diminish the need to perform these functions with a high degree of business competence. These functions include planning, marketing, sales, human resources, business systems, administration, finance, and leadership. Compassion excels in every one of these areas.

In each area Compassion has employed several competent professionals who serve in a leadership capacity and are responsible for the effectiveness with which their area serves the core competency and deliverable of Compassion

International. As in all great companies, the performance of each area and its leaders is measured and evaluated on a regular basis. Appropriate changes are made if and when performance is determined to be marginal and not adequately serving the mission and vision of this ministry.

The stated objective of Compassion International is to grow the number of children being served to five million by the year 2015. The leadership of Compassion recognizes that in order to accomplish this objective, the infrastructure of the ministry would need to be strengthened as part of initiating a significant growth program. This demonstrates that the leadership of this ministry understands The Compound Effect. In order to expand the transformational Kingdom Impact on its ministry the organization must first enhance the business competency and capability of its infrastructure.

> Many ministries try to expand their influence to the nations and the world without adequate preparation.

Many ministries try to expand their influence to the nations and the world without adequate preparation. They never take the time to build the necessary support to achieve their visions consistently over an extended period of time. Instead of investing carefully and diligently for the long term, they scramble for funding and then give their money away in an attempt to achieve their short-term objectives without any consideration for the business aspects of running a ministry.

Compassion International recognizes that in, order to achieve its long-term objectives, they must hire and retain the best people and pay them an appropriate amount according to their skills, abilities, and experience. By doing so Compassion can ensure continuity of culture and a level of credibility within the marketplace that will allow them to raise the necessary funding to support its vision to serve five million children by the year 2015.

FRANK'S STORY

The Lord is constantly blessing me with divine appointments. I met Frank in 2004 through a fellow believer and business owner. The global marketplace has a far greater capacity to transform the lives of people than the corporate church or the multitude of charitable and missions organizations providing their services around the world.

Churches and missions organizations all require funding. For-profit enterprises, owned and operated by spiritually mature Christian business owners, provide their own funding and have the capacity to transform entire communities and nations while at the same time multiplying profits that can be replanted to continue to support their efforts. Frank is one small example of a spiritually mature and incredibly competent Christian businessman whose impact is already being felt around the world.

Frank is a formally trained Dutch industrial design

engineer. At the age of eight Frank gave his heart to the Lord. Frank is an incredibly intelligent, powerfully passionate man of God with a heart for service in the kingdom of God. Shortly before I met Frank he and his wife had moved from Holland to India to establish a start-up business that would employ HIV-positive women. Their mission was to minister to not only the life needs of those women, but also their spiritual, emotional, and medical needs.

Several years ago, in a presentation to a Weavers class, Frank explained in some detail his passion and vision to establish a biblical business legacy for the underprivileged in India. At that point it was just an idea and a vision based on faith. However, it was clearly apparent that Frank had the necessary biblically based business competence, skill, and ability to bring this vision to reality.

He also had a very pragmatic and practical realization of the hurdles and the obstacles that he would encounter. Those hurdles included lack of finance, widespread corruption, and a lack of customers. But Frank had a plan. His vision not only included faith in God, but a detailed step-by-step practical business start-up plan.

Over the next several years we maintained contact through e-mail but never had a chance to reconnect face to face. Then, in May 2009 Frank returned for a visit to the United States. The projected revenue for his company in the next fiscal year is $1.8 million in U.S. dollars. During this particular visit, he met with several professional sports teams to present a very unique promotional item that had been created and manufactured by his company in India. As of this writing, he expects to receive orders for that product from at least two of those teams.

Frank's business is his ministry. The company currently employs forty-two people in India, many of whom are HIV-positive women. The income these employees generate directly supports and affects two hundred fifty additional lives. His company has also successfully established a no-corruption policy. This policy, based on biblical business principles, has been achieved because of Frank's strong leadership and favorable relationship with the Dutch government, who provided a letter indicating that they would not tolerate any corruption in the transactions of this company. This letter of authority has significantly differentiated this company within the business culture of India. As a result of his success, other businesses are now successfully achieving a no-corruption policy. Through God's favor with those in authority, this brand-new Christian business operation has taken a stand against a generational curse of business corruption that has stood unchallenged for hundreds of years in India.

Frank's company employs Hindus, Muslims, and Christians. However, every employee sees and hears the gospel through this business all day, every day. Some have converted, some have not. Yet in every case their standard of living has improved dramatically, their stature in the community has been enhanced beyond anything that they could have accomplished on their own, and their influence within their families and their communities is significantly greater. The goal of the company is to grow to $15 million in annual revenues and 250 employees by 2012.

Once again, this is business as ministry. This company is creating Kingdom Impact through the marketplace by adhering to what Weavers has identified as biblical business leadership commitments. I was led to encourage Frank to realize that the small seeds he is sowing in India today as a Christian business owner will bear massive amounts of fruit through multiple generations to come. God is using Frank mightily to change the face of the business community and the social and spiritual conditions of those within his sphere of influence. In his lifetime he will make a major contribution to changing the face of that nation. He will transform lives and generate incredible profits and resources all at the same time. This is The Compound Effect in action.

CHAPTER 11

THE MARK OF GREATNESS

For our struggle is not against flesh
and blood, but against the rulers, against
the authorities, against the powers of
this dark world and against the spiritual
forces of evil in the heavenly realms.

— Ephesians 6:12

Great businesses and ministries recognize that lean times and recessions (famine) are inevitable. In the past thirty years we have seen the U.S. economy rise and fall at least four times. The global economy is constantly in turmoil and never uniformly predictable as it continuously reacts to the influence of political instability and upheaval. Great businesses plan and prepare during the good times so they can continue to serve their constituencies when the famine arrives. Businesses and ministries that are operated with competence and spiritual maturity actually thrive and prosper in adverse times, while others fail. The Scriptures offer vibrant lessons about how we need to prepare for the "famine" seasons of life.

> *Businesses and ministries that are operated with competence and spiritual maturity actually thrive and prosper in adverse times, while others fail.*

Joseph was thirty years old when he entered the service of Pharaoh king of Egypt. And Joseph went out from Pharaoh's presence and traveled throughout Egypt. During the seven years of abundance the land produced plentifully. Joseph collected all the food produced in those seven years of abundance in Egypt and stored it in the cities. In each city he put the food grown in the fields surrounding it. Joseph stored up huge quantities of grain, like the sand of the sea; it was so much that he stopped keeping records because it was beyond measure. . . .

When the famine had spread over the whole country, Joseph opened the storehouses and sold grain to the Egyptians, for the famine was severe throughout Egypt. And all the countries came to Egypt to buy grain from Joseph, because the famine was severe in all the world.

—Genesis 41:46-49,56-57

Joseph was prepared to manage the famine. God saw to it that he had the training and preparation to do the job that was entrusted to him by Pharaoh. Joseph's business competence (wisdom installed and anointed in him by God) placed him in a unique position to influence the culture of a nation.

Within the context of The Compound Effect, Joseph became a spiritual leader through his dependence and recognition of the power of God. However, at the same time, he also developed his business and administrative competence to a significant level. The Lord also saw to it that he had the business and leadership skills to manage the people and logistics to execute the Pharaoh's "famine management" plan in accordance with God's design. Twenty years passed between the time Joseph was sold into slavery until the time the famine began. God had a lifetime plan for Joseph that required twenty years of preparation—just to get started. How many businesses today have a twenty-year start-up plan? Raising a child is a twenty-year process, so why shouldn't starting and building a strong business or ministry involve the same commitment?

A Modern-Day Joseph

Greg is a prominent Christian real estate developer and a stockholder and board member of a local bank. He is well known and respected for his philanthropic efforts and his generous giving to various ministries. Over the past twenty years Greg has developed a number of large parcels of residential and commercial property in the community. But the current economy has severely limited his development business. He has been forced to reduce his staff and limit his activities to managing his existing inventory of properties.

Greg currently has $8 million in liquid assets. Over the past twenty-four months he has been diligently seeking a financing package to commercially develop two new parcels of land. Because of the circumstances of the current economy he has been unable to find a financial institution willing to finance projects unless he provides 50 percent of the funding. In the past, all of his projects have been funded by financial institutions with a 20 percent equity position. Each one of those prior projects was profitable and Greg and his wife have given generously from those profits.

Greg and his wife are currently living and tithing from the interest generated by their $8 million capital fund. All of the revenues being generated by his real estate holdings are enabling him to maintain his current staff and keep them employed. That $8 million fund is Greg's seed capital and he is unwilling and unable at this point to support any new ministries from those dollars that are set aside to fund future projects. As he said, "This is our seed."

One of Greg's proposed commercial projects requires $9 million in cash, of which he must provide $2.7 million of his own money. That project will take at least five years to complete and should generate in excess of $20 million in revenues. Greg's business plan includes $3 million in philanthropic gifts to ministries. However, if he were to commit that $3 million today from his current nest egg, he would not be in a position to even consider this project.

After thirty years of hard work and diligent perseverance to build his current "seed capital fund," Greg's heart is to continue to serve the kingdom through his business by providing financial resources to worthwhile ministries. But without this financial nest egg, his ability to support ministries in the future would be nonexistent. The Lord has provided this resource and Greg knows that he must steward it in such a way that it is multiplied and not wasted.

Greg has always had a unique gift to look into the future and see opportunities well before anyone else recognized them. He was also provided the gift of patience, which is absolutely essential to be a successful developer. Sometimes the best thing to do in his business is wait.

He has been well rewarded for his patience, even though there were many times when he thought that he had waited too long, or perhaps not long enough.

Greg is a living, breathing example of The Compound Effect, the transformational power of business competency and spiritual maturity. Greg did not arrive at his current station in life by accident. He worked hard. He took risks. He made mistakes. He learned from his mistakes. He studied the Word. He prayed. He sought wise counsel. He worked hard. He built a personal relationship with the Lord. He purposed to serve God through his business. Greg's business competency will continue to have, through future generations, profound transformational impact in God's kingdom.

Seeking to Improve

So how do we grow our business competency? First, we need to honestly ask ourselves: "What is our current level of business competency?" As you read through the descriptions in chapters 7 and 8, no doubt you were evaluating your own level of business competency. You should be asking yourself, "Where do I fall within these behaviors that reflect the various levels of business competency? Is my business in the survivor, successful, or significant mode? Am I a survivor, successful, or significant business leader?

You have the opportunity to assess your business skills on the Weavers website using our competency assessment tool, at **www.weaversonline.org/assessments**. This tool will enable you to perform a subjective and accurate self-assessment, provided you answer with absolute honesty and transparency as you respond to our questions. Remember to approach the questions prayerfully, as God knows our hearts better than we do.

Building true "wisdom" (business competence) requires time. Knowledge plus skill plus experience plus time yields competence. Gaining experience implies that you work at a skill through multiple failures until you consistently achieve a level of proficiency.

How do we also build spiritual maturity? Growing spiritual maturity works much the same way as building business competence. As we did with business competence we need to ask ourselves, *Where am I today with my spiritual maturity?* As you read through the descriptions in chapter 5, did you check your own level of spiritual maturity? Did you ask yourself, *Where do I fall within these behaviors that reflect the various levels of spiritual maturity?* Are you a user, a servant, or a leader?

The spiritual maturity assessment tool is also provided for you online at **www.weaversonline.org/assessments**. This tool will enable you to perform a self-assessment of your current level of spiritual maturity that is equally subjective.

To improve our spiritual maturity, we need to prayerfully and intentionally work to modify our behaviors to become more Christlike in our daily living. We need to ask ourselves several critical questions to help this process:

What behaviors actually reflect my spiritual maturity?

What behaviors do I need to improve to advance my spiritual maturity?

How does my language need to change to reflect spiritual maturity?

What actions need to change to reflect spiritual maturity?

The family is God's vehicle for generational blessing. The fruit of spiritual maturity will be harvested within your family first. Spiritual maturity will have no fruit if it does not serve the family first. What are the legacies you desire to leave with your family?

There have been numerous successful businesses owned by Christians where the legacy within the family was defined by heartache and destruction because the spiritual maturity of the father (or mother) and founder of the business never went beyond a "user." It was always about him (or her). His choice was to place a higher priority on building his business competence than to shepherd his family. There was no effort to maintain a daily Bible study and prayer time, embrace a servant leader attitude, acknowledge the sovereignty of God, or develop a humble attitude of accountability. Despite the best human intentions and endless physical and emotional sacrifices, these business stories are littered with broken marriages, broken family relationships, and businesses that just evaporate for lack of spiritual maturity.

The choice to improve spiritual maturity is not an easy one. It starts with several basic decisions that all seem counterintuitive to an entrepreneur.

1. I am willing to submit to God's will for my life; I am no longer in charge.
2. I will commit to daily Bible study and prayer.
3. I am the steward, not the owner, of my business. Everything I own is ultimately God's.
4. My first priority is to love God with all my heart, soul, mind and strength.
5. My family's spiritual condition is a higher priority than my business.

Now that you have determined your level of business competency and spiritual maturity, you can apply The Compound Effect and multiply those two factors together to determine the current level of the Kingdom Impact of your business (**www.weaversonline.org/assessments**).

Over the rest of your life you can continue to use The Compound Effect to determine if you are improving your Kingdom Impact and creating increasing levels of Christ-honoring transformation in the lives of those in your sphere of influence.

A Lifetime Legacy

How much time is needed to grow your business competency and spiritual maturity and establish a legacy of wealth and resources for the kingdom of God? The short answer is: a lifetime. There are no shortcuts. There is no "easy" paint-by-numbers solution. The problem is many people set about to write a business plan and start a new business before they have a life plan. That is not what God intends. *If you have a business plan before you have a life plan, your business will become your life!*

If your life plan is not in order, do not start a new business. If you are going to own a business, then it should be the vehicle to get you to God's destination for your life. This also applies to ministries. People who work with and for ministries should have a life plan and the ministry should operate in concert with that life plan. Ministries that fail to recognize and serve the life needs of their staff, employees, and volunteers will not only cause adverse impact on the body of Christ, but will ultimately fail in their mission.

We will all leave a legacy. Will your legacy be vital and life giving, or will it be a continuous curse to future generations? What are the legacies you expect to leave behind? The twenty-eighth chapter of Deuteronomy offers specific long-term benefits for honoring the Lord's commands. But this Scripture also paints a vivid picture of the costs to be paid by future generations for violating God's laws.

If you do not carefully follow all the words of this law, which are written in this book, and do not revere this glorious and awesome name—the L<small>ORD</small> your God—the L<small>ORD</small> will send fearful plagues on you and your descendants, harsh and prolonged disasters, and severe and lingering illnesses.

—Deuteronomy 28:58-59

Godly stewardship multiplies legacies from one generation to the next. It takes four types of "seed capital" to build and leave a legacy. Leaving a legacy is not just about finances. Generational legacy also requires three other key forms of capital in addition to finances.

> Godly stewardship multiplies legacies from one generation to the next.

Spiritual capital passed from one generation to another serves as the moral compass for godly stewardship of resources. Intellectual capital is the practical wisdom, knowledge, and discernment on how to deploy legacy resources. And, finally, sustaining legacy through generations requires social capital, or "leadership"—the ability to build and sustain relationships. We have seen many financial legacies destroyed for lack of spiritual, intellectual, or social capital. Massive potential resources for the kingdom of God have been wasted through moral, intellectual, and social incompetence.

Moving Forward

What choices do you need to make today? What action steps do you need to take? If you are in business and do not have a life plan, take the time to write one. If you are not certain of your gift or calling, spend some time prayerfully seeking the Lord about how He has designed you. There are numerous analytical tools available online at **www.followyourcalling.com** to help with that process. But here are some very basic questions you can ask to achieve a better understanding of how to prepare yourself to establish or operate a thriving business for the Lord's purposes:

1. What am I really passionate about?
2. Am I task or goal oriented?
3. What am I *not* good at? (Sometimes the process of elimination can be very insightful.)
4. How do I learn? By doing? By watching? By hearing?
5. How do I feel about risk? (If you are risk averse, being a business owner may not be for you.)
6. How can I best serve others? How do I relate to others?
7. If money was not an issue, what would I do?
8. What is the highest priority in my life?
9. What life experiences have defined me?
10. Who do I admire?
11. Who and what am I responsible for?

I am constantly amazed by how the Lord shapes and forms us through our life's experiences to expose and expand our gifts and callings when we make it a priority to serve His purposes and adhere to His principles. However, be warned, the process of understanding and fully flowing in your gift takes years and diligence on your part. Great talent or skill clothed in arrogance is useless to the Lord. Quiet humility without relevant skill or ability is equally worthless.

Make a choice today to actively improve your business competency and spiritual maturity. Not just today, but every day for the rest of your life. Read the Word. Pray. Test God. Trust God. If you are a business owner or feel the Lord has called you to be a business owner, make a choice today to build your business skills and competencies every day. Commit to constant learning and improvement for yourself and your organization. Commit to follow The Compound Effect road map to transformational Kingdom Impact.

As a Christian business owner, what is the outcome the Lord expects from you and your business—today, this month, this year, this decade, and this lifetime? God expects the complete transformation of the lives of the people within your sphere of influence. He expects Christ to be reflected in your thoughts, actions, and deeds. He expects forgiveness and unconditional love. He expects godly stewardship over the lives and resources that He has entrusted to you. He expects courage and conviction in the face of opposition. He expects faith and perseverance in the face of adversity. He expects discipline and determination in daily devotion to Him.

Be careful to follow every command I am giving you today, so that you may live and increase and may enter and possess the land that the LORD promised on oath to your forefathers. . . .You may say to yourself, "My power and the strength of my hands have produced this wealth for me." But remember the LORD your God, for it is he who gives you the ability to produce

wealth, and so confirms his covenant, which he swore
to your forefathers, as it is today. If you ever forget
the LORD your God and follow other gods and worship
and bow down to them, I testify against you today
that you will surely be destroyed.

—Deuteronomy 8:1,17-19

The Lord has entrusted some with the ability to create wealth. However, the penalty for allowing that wealth to consume us is that we will forfeit it and be destroyed. He requires an exceptionally high standard of commitment, loyalty, and integrity from those He has chosen to accumulate and steward His wealth. Many have the gift to produce wealth, but few have the spiritual maturity to sustain and multiply it generationally.

The Lord is ultimately the owner of all wealth. However, in our current age there are not enough spiritually mature, skilled, and competent business owners willing and able to steward that wealth for the Lord's transformational purposes. I would prayerfully challenge you, that if you know your gift and calling is to create wealth, to follow our road map. Commit to the constant improvement of your business competency while you submit yourself to the Lord in humility so He can grow your spiritual maturity. Your business competency multiplied by your spiritual maturity will create incredible transformational Kingdom Impact for generations to come.

THE COMPOUND EFFECT

CONTINUE TO GROW IN BUSINESS COMPETENCY & SPIRITUAL MATURITY

The author is available for speaking engagements, business as ministry training, and one on one direct business consultation. Contact us at **TCEtraining@weaversonline.org** for additional training and materials on the ideas and concepts contained in this book, including:

◆ presentations on The Compound Effect,

◆ intensive one-day Compound Effect Training workshops,

◆ extended classroom courses or business consulting for your business, ministry, or church

strengthening the fabric of your business